HERSHEY'S
CHOCOLATE
CLASSICS

All About Chocolate _____ 2

Showstoppers _____ 6

Cakes & Cheesecakes _____ 16

Pies & Pastries _____ 35

Cookies & Bar Cookies _____ 46

Puddings, Mousses & Soufflés _____ 56

Candies _____ 66

Breads & Coffeecakes _____ 73

Microwave Specialties _____ 80

Sauces & Frostings _____ 88

Index _____ 94

All About Chocolate

An "original American," the cacao bean was one of the treasures Columbus brought back from the New World. But neither he nor his patrons, Ferdinand and Isabella of Spain, understood its potential pleasures. It took Cortez, while conquering Mexico for Spain, to realize that there must be something very special about this *chocoatl* if Emperor Montezuma and his Aztec court sipped it from golden goblets.

Golden goblets notwithstanding, the rich chocolate liquid was not to Spanish tastes until someone added a bit of sugar and a drop or so of vanilla, heated the mixture and topped it with a cinnamon stick. With that, chocolate became the "in" drink of the day in Spain. Eventually, chocolate fever spread to Italy, then to France and Holland and finally to England. There its popularity was so great that there were actually Chocolate Houses, where meeting, greeting and sipping were the order of the day.

Chocolate, however, was still considered exotic. It was also quite expensive, as the cacao beans were still grown, picked and processed much as they had been in Cortez's time. During the Industrial Revolution, methods were developed to make chocolate finer and smoother. But perhaps the biggest step toward chocolate as we know it today was taken in Switzerland in the 1800s, when Daniel Peter added milk to basic chocolate. He also developed the formula for making the first solid chocolate. Chocolate finally sailed back across the Atlantic, and it was Milton S. Hershey who made it a true All-American.

Chocolate and Hershey have been virtually synonymous since the turn of the century, when Milton Hershey built his chocolate factory amid the rich dairylands of Pennsylvania's Lebanon Valley. It's an association that's even stronger today, and one that we're very proud of.

Over the years, thousands upon thousands of chocolate recipes have been developed and tested in the Hershey Kitchens. The following pages feature more than 100 of the recipes that we deem to be the very best. Many of them will doubtless remind you of your favorite childhood chocolate treats; others will introduce you to imaginative new ways to enjoy chocolate and cocoa in all their delicious forms. We hope you will enjoy sampling the wide variety of recipes offered for every taste and for every occasion.

CHOCOLATE IS CHOCOLATE...OR IS IT?

Purists would limit the use of the word "chocolate" to just two forms: solid unsweetened chocolate or its liquid form, chocolate liquor. They're right, of course. But the rest of the world is happily willing to accept a much broader definition. Here's a little background on chocolate in its various phases and forms:

Cacao (Cocoa) Beans are the starting point. They are the fruit of the cacao tree, which grows in a very limited climate zone—only 20 degrees north and south of the Equator—and mainly in West Africa and Latin America.

Cacao Nibs are the "meat" of the beans. The beans are cleaned and then roasted at carefully controlled temperatures to bring out their full flavor and aroma. When the outer shells are removed, the nibs are ready to go on to greater things. (They contain more than 50% cocoa butter, and that's rich treasure indeed.)

Chocolate Liquor is what makes all real chocolate products possible. The nibs are ground by a process that generates enough heat to liquefy the cocoa butter, thus creating the liquor. (The term "liquor" is used in its true sense, that of liquid essence—it has nothing to do with alcohol.)

Cocoa Butter is the vegetable fat that's extracted when the chocolate liquor is "pressed" under high pressure. This butter has a distinctive melting quality that gives chocolate products their unique texture.

Cocoa Powder made by the American process (such as HERSHEY'S Cocoa) is the marvelous by-product that remains after most of the cocoa butter has been extracted from the liquor. It has no additives and no preservatives, so it's 100% pure. And because most of the cocoa butter has been removed, it has the lowest fat content of any chocolate product. Stored in a tightly closed container, cocoa will retain its freshness and quality almost indefinitely—and without refrigeration.

Dutch-Process Cocoa Powder is made from chocolate liquor that has been treated with an alkali agent. This makes a darker powder, with a flavor that differs from that of American-process cocoa.

Bitter Chocolate, commonly referred to as unsweetened, baking or cooking chocolate, is chocolate *au naturel*. It is pure chocolate liquor, cooled and molded, usually in blocks.

Semi-Sweet Chocolate is a combination of chocolate liquor with added cocoa butter and sugar. To qualify for this term, the product must contain at least 35% chocolate liquor. Available in bars, this form is more popularly available in chips.

Sweet (Dark) Chocolate combines the same ingredients as semi-sweet, but the balance is different. This form must contain at least 15% chocolate liquor, but it has a higher sugar level.

Milk Chocolate also uses the same ingredients but with the addition of milk or cream. At least 10% chocolate liquor is required in milk chocolate products.

White Chocolate, also called confectioners' chocolate, is known in the chocolate industry as compound chocolate. It isn't really chocolate at all. Most or all of the cocoa butter has been removed and replaced by another vegetable fat, and it contains no chocolate liquor. Also called confectioners' coating, it is available in a range of colors, from dark to white and even pastels.

Chocolate-Flavored is the term applied to food products that derive their flavor from cocoa and/or chocolate liquor but do not contain a sufficient quantity of these ingredients to meet the government's definition of "true" chocolate. Chocolate-flavored syrups, which combine chocolate liquor or cocoa, sugar, water, salt and sometimes other flavorings, are among the products that fall under this category.

Artificial Chocolate is a product of the chemical industry, not chocolate-makers. Such products contain no ingredients derived from the cacao bean—and, at the extreme, contain no sugar or milk.

MELTING CHOCOLATE

Using a Double Boiler: This is the preferred method for melting all types of chocolate, avoiding both scorching and the formation of steam droplets. Simply place chocolate blocks or chocolate chips in the top of a double boiler over hot, not boiling, water.

Using Direct Heat: Because chocolate scorches so easily, this method is not strongly recommended. There are three "musts": very low heat; a heavy saucepan; constant stirring.

Using a Microwave Oven: Note that in the microwave oven, chocolate blocks and chips will keep their shape even when they are softened. Stir to determine whether chocolate is fluid and melted.

• *Unsweetened Baking Chocolate and Semi-Sweet Baking Chocolate:* Unwrap, break blocks in half and place desired amount in micro-proof measuring cup or bowl. Microwave at HIGH (100%) for half the minimum time listed below; stir. Continue to microwave until chocolate is softened; stir. Allow to stand several minutes to finish melting; stir again. (If unmelted chocolate still remains, return to microwave and heat for an additional 30 seconds; stir until fluid.)

1 block (1 ounce)	1 to 1½ minutes
2 blocks (2 ounces)	1½ to 2 minutes
3 blocks (3 ounces)	2 to 2½ minutes
4 blocks (4 ounces)	2½ to 3 minutes

• *Chips (Semi-Sweet, Milk, MINI CHIPS Chocolates or Peanut Butter):* Place 1 cup (about 6 ounces) chips in 2-cup micro-proof measuring cup or bowl. Microwave at HIGH (100%) for 1 to 1½ minutes or until softened; stir. Allow to stand for several minutes to finish melting; stir until smooth.

For Small Amounts: If melting less than 2 ounces, place in a small heatproof cup. Place small amount of warm water in a shallow pan; set cup in pan. Stir chocolate until smooth. (Or use a microwave oven.)

Tips from the Experts
• Wash and dry the melting utensil thoroughly after each use. Any residue will affect the flavor of chocolate.
• A wet utensil or the condensation of steam droplets can cause chocolate to get stiff and grainy. Don't panic. As an emergency measure, stir in 1 teaspoon solid vegetable shortening (not butter) for every 2 ounces of chocolate.
• Stir the melting chocolate periodically with a wire whisk to help blending and discourage scorching.
• Break chocolate into 1-inch pieces to speed the melting process.

STORING CHOCOLATE

Chocolate products will stay fresh for well over a year if stored in a cool, dry place (65°–70°F). It's best to keep an eye on temperature and humidity.

Temperatures above 78°F will cause chocolate to melt. The cocoa butter then rises to the surface and forms a grayish discoloration called "cocoa butter bloom." Condensation on milk or semi-sweet chocolate may cause the sugar to dissolve and rise to the surface as "sugar bloom." Neither "bloom" affects the quality or flavor of chocolate and, once melted, the chocolate will regain its original color. Thus, it's a good idea to keep chocolate (well wrapped, of course) in as cool a place as possible during prolonged periods of heat and high humidity.

USING COCOA INSTEAD OF CHOCOLATE

Cocoa is so convenient to use that many cooks use it as a substitute for chocolate in their favorite recipes. Here's an easy formula:

For unsweetened baking chocolate: 3 level tablespoons cocoa plus 1 tablespoon shortening (liquid or solid) equals 1 block (1 ounce).

For premelted unsweetened chocolate: 3 tablespoons cocoa plus 1 tablespoon oil or melted shortening equals 1 envelope (1 ounce).

For semi-sweet chocolate: 6 tablespoons cocoa plus 7 tablespoons sugar plus ¼ cup shortening equals one 6-ounce package (1 cup) semi-sweet chocolate chips or 6 blocks (1 ounce each) semi-sweet chocolate.

For sweet baking chocolate: 3 tablespoons cocoa plus 4½ tablespoons sugar plus 2⅔ tablespoons shortening equals 1 bar (4 ounces).

A Note About Butter or Margarine

Regular butter or margarine in sticks should be used in Hershey recipes. Diet, soft, "light," and vegetable oil spread products act differently in cooking and baking than regular butter or stick margarine and may cause unsatisfactory results.

Showstoppers

CRÈME DE CACAO TORTE

⅔ cup butter or margarine, softened
1⅔ cups sugar
3 eggs
½ teaspoon vanilla
2 cups unsifted all-purpose flour
⅔ cup HERSHEY'S Cocoa

1¼ teaspoons baking soda
¼ teaspoon baking powder
1⅓ cups milk
2 tablespoons crème de cacao
Crème de Cacao Filling
Chocolate Ganache Glaze

Cream butter, sugar, eggs and vanilla in large mixer bowl until light and fluffy. Combine flour, cocoa, baking soda and baking powder; add alternately with milk to creamed mixture, blending just until combined.

Pour into two greased and floured 9-inch layer pans. Bake at 350° for 30 to 35 minutes or until cake tester comes out clean. Cool 10 minutes; remove from pans. Sprinkle each layer with 1 tablespoon crème de cacao; cool completely.

Meanwhile, prepare Crème de Cacao Filling. Split each cake layer horizontally into 2 layers. Place one layer on serving plate; spread with one-third of the filling. Repeat layering with remaining cake and filling, ending with cake layer. Cover tightly; chill at least 8 hours. Prepare Chocolate Ganache Glaze; spoon on top of chilled cake, allowing glaze to drizzle down side. Chill. Garnish as desired.   *10 to 12 servings*

CRÈME DE CACAO FILLING

1 cup heavy or whipping cream
2 tablespoons crème de cacao

1 tablespoon HERSHEY'S Cocoa

Beat cream, crème de cacao and cocoa until stiff. Cover; chill.

(continued)

Crème de Cacao Torte

CHOCOLATE GANACHE GLAZE

1 HERSHEY'S SPECIAL DARK Sweet Chocolate Bar (8 ounces), broken into pieces

¹/₄ cup heavy or whipping cream
1 tablespoon butter or margarine
1¹/₂ teaspoons crème de cacao

Combine chocolate bar pieces, cream and butter in medium saucepan. Cook over low heat, stirring constantly, until mixture is melted and smooth. Stir in crème de cacao. Cool to lukewarm (glaze will be slightly thickened).

Pears au Chocolat

PEARS AU CHOCOLAT

4 fresh pears
½ cup sugar
1 cup water
1 teaspoon vanilla
6 tablespoons finely chopped
    nuts

2 tablespoons confectioners'
    sugar
1 teaspoon milk
Chocolate Sauce

Core pears from bottom, leaving stems intact. Peel pears. Slice piece off bottom to make a flat base. Combine sugar and water in medium saucepan; add pears. Cover; simmer over low heat 10 to 20 minutes (depending on ripeness) or just until pears are soft. Remove from heat; add vanilla. Cool pears in syrup; chill. Combine nuts, confectioners' sugar and milk in small bowl. To serve, drain pears; spoon nut mixture into cavities. Place pears on dessert plates. Prepare Chocolate Sauce; pour or spoon sauce onto each pear. Serve with remaining sauce.   *4 servings*

CHOCOLATE SAUCE

6 tablespoons water
6 tablespoons sugar
¼ cup butter or margarine

1⅓ cups HERSHEY'S MINI CHIPS
    Semi-Sweet Chocolate

Combine water, sugar and butter in small saucepan; bring to full boil. Remove from heat; stir in MINI CHIPS Chocolates. Stir until chocolate has completely melted; beat or whisk until smooth. Cool.

PEANUT BUTTER SHELLS
WITH CHOCOLATE-ALMOND CREAM

2 cups (12-ounce package)
REESE'S Peanut Butter Chips
2 tablespoons shortening*

Chocolate-Almond Cream
Filling

Melt peanut butter chips and shortening in top of double boiler over hot, not boiling, water; stir until smooth. Remove from heat; cool slightly. Place 15 paper baking cups (2³/₄ inches in diameter) in muffin pans. Using a narrow, soft-bristled pastry brush, thickly and evenly coat the inside pleated surface and bottom of each cup with peanut butter mixture. (Reserve any remaining peanut butter mixture for touch-up.) Chill 10 minutes; coat any thin spots. (If peanut butter mixture thickens, stir over hot water until mixture becomes fluid again.) Cover; chill at least 1 hour or until firm.

Remove only a few peanut butter shells from refrigerator at a time; carefully peel paper from each cup. (Unfilled cups will keep for weeks in an airtight container in the refrigerator.) Fill each cup with Chocolate-Almond Cream Filling; chill several hours or overnight.   *15 desserts*

*Do not use butter, margarine or oil.

CHOCOLATE-ALMOND CREAM FILLING

1 HERSHEY'S Milk Chocolate
Bar with Almonds
(8 ounces)
1¹/₂ cups miniature or 15 large
marshmallows

¹/₃ cup milk
1 cup heavy or whipping cream

Cut chocolate bar in pieces, chopping almonds into small pieces. Place in top of double boiler and melt with marshmallows and milk over hot, not boiling, water. Stir until chocolate and marshmallows are melted and mixture is smooth. Remove from heat; cool. Whip cream until stiff and fold into chocolate mixture. Cover; chill until ready to use.

Tip: You may prepare the shells weeks in advance of use, but for best results make the filling no earlier than a day ahead of serving time.

CHOCO-COCONUT CAKE ROLL

4 egg whites, at room
   temperature
$1/2$ cup sugar
4 egg yolks, at room temperature
$1/3$ cup sugar
1 teaspoon vanilla
$1/2$ cup unsifted all-purpose flour

$1/3$ cup HERSHEY'S Cocoa
$1/2$ teaspoon baking powder
$1/4$ teaspoon baking soda
$1/8$ teaspoon salt
$1/3$ cup water
Cherry-Coconut Filling
Confectioners' sugar

Line $15^1/2 \times 10^1/2 \times 1$-inch jelly roll pan with aluminum foil; generously grease foil. Set aside. Beat egg whites in large mixer bowl until foamy; gradually add $1/2$ cup sugar and beat until stiff peaks form. Set aside.

Beat egg yolks in small mixer bowl 3 minutes on high speed. Gradually add $1/3$ cup sugar and the vanilla; continue beating 2 additional minutes. Combine flour, cocoa, baking powder, baking soda and salt; add alternately with water to egg yolk mixture, beating on low speed just until batter is smooth. Gradually fold chocolate mixture into beaten egg whites until mixture is well blended.

Spread batter evenly in prepared pan. Bake at 375° for 12 to 15 minutes or until cake springs back when touched lightly. Invert onto towel sprinkled with confectioners' sugar; carefully peel off foil. Immediately roll cake and towel together starting from narrow end; place on wire rack to cool completely.

Prepare Cherry-Coconut Filling. Carefully unroll cake; remove towel. Spread cake with filling; reroll and chill. Sprinkle with confectioners' sugar just before serving.   *8 to 10 servings*

CHERRY-COCONUT FILLING

1 cup heavy or whipping cream
3 tablespoons confectioners'
   sugar
Few drops red food color
   (optional)

$1/3$ cup chopped maraschino
   cherries, well drained
$1/2$ cup flaked coconut

Beat cream until slightly thickened. Add confectioners' sugar and food color; beat until stiff. Fold in cherries and coconut.

Choco-Coconut Cake Roll

GEORGIA PEACH SHORTCAKE

4 egg yolks
½ cup sugar
½ cup unsifted all-purpose flour
⅓ cup HERSHEY'S Cocoa
¼ cup sugar
½ teaspoon baking soda
¼ teaspoon salt
⅓ cup water

1 teaspoon vanilla
4 egg whites
2 tablespoons sugar
2 cups heavy or whipping cream
¾ cup confectioners' sugar
1 teaspoon vanilla
3 cups sliced peaches, well
   drained*

Grease bottom of two 9-inch square or layer pans. Line with wax paper; grease paper. Set aside. Beat egg yolks 3 minutes on medium speed in large mixer bowl. Gradually add ½ cup sugar; continue beating 2 minutes. Combine flour, cocoa, ¼ cup sugar, the baking soda and salt; add alternately with water and 1 teaspoon vanilla on low speed just until batter is smooth. Beat egg whites in small mixer bowl until foamy; add 2 tablespoons sugar and beat until stiff peaks form. Carefully fold beaten egg whites into chocolate mixture.

Spread batter evenly in prepared pans. Bake at 375° for 14 to 16 minutes or until cake springs back when touched lightly. Cool 10 minutes; remove cakes from pans. Peel off wax paper; cool completely.

Beat cream, confectioners' sugar and 1 teaspoon vanilla in large mixer bowl until stiff. Place one cake layer upside down on serving plate; frost with about 1 cup of the whipped cream. With pastry tube or spoon, make a border of whipped cream ½ inch high and 1 inch wide around edge of layer. Fill center with peach slices, reserving 12 peach slices for top of cake. Carefully place second layer, top side up, on filling. Gently spread all but 1 cup whipped cream on top of cake. With pastry tube or spoon, make a border of whipped cream around edge of top layer of cake. Arrange remaining peach slices in center. Chill about 1 hour before serving. *10 to 12 servings*

*Use fresh peaches or 16-ounce package frozen or 29-ounce can peach slices.

Georgia Peach Shortcake

Mexican Cocoa Torte

MEXICAN COCOA TORTE

1 cup sugar
1/2 cup HERSHEY'S Cocoa
1/4 teaspoon cinnamon
1/3 cup shortening
1/2 cup strong coffee
1 package (11 ounces) pie crust
   mix

2 cups heavy or whipping cream
HERSHEY'S MINI CHIPS
   Semi-Sweet Chocolate
   (optional)

Combine sugar, cocoa, cinnamon, shortening and coffee in small saucepan. Cook over very low heat, stirring constantly, until smooth and creamy. Cool to room temperature. Place pie crust mix in medium mixing bowl; stir in 3/4 cup of the cocoa mixture, blending thoroughly. Shape into smooth ball; chill 1 hour.

Divide dough into 4 pieces. Line two cookie sheets with aluminum foil; mark two 8-inch circles on each. Place balls of dough on foil; press with fingers into marked circles. Bake at 375° for 10 to 12 minutes or until almost set; cool on cookie sheets.

Add remaining cocoa mixture to cream in small mixer bowl; beat until stiff. Place one pastry round on serving plate; spread with one-fourth of the whipped cream mixture. Repeat layering with remaining three rounds and whipped cream mixture, ending with whipped cream. Chill several hours. Garnish with MINI CHIPS Chocolates. *8 to 10 servings*

HEAVENLY HEART CAKE

3/4 cup HERSHEY'S Cocoa
2/3 cup boiling water
3/4 cup butter or margarine,
　softened
2 cups sugar
1 teaspoon vanilla
2 eggs
2 cups unsifted cake flour or
　1 3/4 cups unsifted all-purpose
　flour

1 1/4 teaspoons baking soda
1/4 teaspoon salt
3/4 cup buttermilk or sour milk*
　Glossy Chocolate Sour Cream
　　Frosting
　Creamy Buttercream Frosting

Stir together cocoa and boiling water in small bowl until smooth; set aside. Cream butter, sugar and vanilla in large mixer bowl until light and fluffy; beat in eggs and cocoa mixture. Combine flour, baking soda and salt; add alternately with buttermilk to creamed mixture.

Line bottom of two heart-shaped pans with wax paper. Pour batter into prepared pans. Bake at 350° for 30 to 35 minutes or until cake tester comes out clean. Cool 10 minutes; remove from pans. Cool completely. Frost with Glossy Chocolate Sour Cream Frosting and decorate as desired with Creamy Buttercream Frosting.　　　　　　　　　　　　　*8 to 10 servings*

*To sour milk: Use 2 teaspoons vinegar plus milk to equal 3/4 cup.

Note: If you don't have heart-shaped pans, bake cake as directed in two greased and floured pans: a 9-inch square and a 9-inch round. Slice round layer in half; arrange halves beside square layer to form heart shape.

GLOSSY CHOCOLATE SOUR CREAM FROSTING

1 1/2 cups HERSHEY'S Semi-Sweet
　　Chocolate Chips
3/4 cup sour cream

2 cups confectioners' sugar
1 teaspoon vanilla

Melt chocolate chips in top of double boiler over hot, not boiling, water, stirring constantly until completely melted. Remove from heat; beat in sour cream, confectioners' sugar and vanilla.

CREAMY BUTTERCREAM FROSTING

2 cups confectioners' sugar
1/4 cup butter or margarine,
　softened

2 1/2 tablespoons milk
1/2 teaspoon vanilla
Few drops red food color

Combine confectioners' sugar, butter, milk, vanilla and food color in small bowl until smooth and creamy.

Top: Heavenly Heart Cake
Bottom: Holiday Chocolate Cookies (see page 54)

Cakes & Cheesecakes

COCOA-SPICE SNACKIN' CAKE

¹/₄ cup butter or margarine, melted	³/₄ teaspoon baking soda
¹/₄ cup HERSHEY'S Cocoa	¹/₂ teaspoon cinnamon
³/₄ cup applesauce	¹/₄ teaspoon nutmeg
1¹/₄ cups unsifted all-purpose flour	¹/₄ teaspoon salt
1 cup sugar	1 egg, beaten
	¹/₂ cup chopped nuts

Combine melted butter and cocoa; blend in applesauce. Combine flour, sugar, baking soda, cinnamon, nutmeg and salt in large bowl. Blend in cocoa mixture and egg until dry ingredients are moistened. Stir in nuts.

Spread in greased 9-inch square pan. Bake at 350° for 30 to 35 minutes or until cake tester comes out clean. Cool in pan.   *8 to 10 servings*

CHOCOLATETOWN SPECIAL CAKE

¹/₂ cup HERSHEY'S Cocoa	2 eggs
¹/₂ cup boiling water	2¹/₄ cups unsifted all-purpose flour
²/₃ cup shortening	1¹/₂ teaspoons baking soda
1³/₄ cups sugar	¹/₂ teaspoon salt
1 teaspoon vanilla	1¹/₃ cups buttermilk or sour milk*

(continued)

*To sour milk: Use 4 teaspoons vinegar plus milk to equal 1¹/₃ cups.

Chocolatetown Special Cake with Chocolate Fudge Frosting (see page 92)

Stir together cocoa and boiling water in small bowl until smooth; set aside. Cream shortening, sugar and vanilla in large mixer bowl until light and fluffy. Add eggs; beat well. Combine flour, baking soda and salt; add alternately with buttermilk to creamed mixture. Blend in cocoa mixture.

Pour into three greased and floured 8-inch or two 9-inch layer pans. Bake at 350° for 25 to 30 minutes for 8-inch pans or 35 to 40 minutes for 9-inch pans, or until cake tester comes out clean. Cool 10 minutes; remove from pans. Cool completely; frost as desired (see pages 88–93).   *8 to 10 servings*

NO-BAKE CHOCOLATE CHEESECAKE

Crumb-Nut Crust
1½ cups HERSHEY'S Semi-Sweet
  Chocolate Chips
1 package (8 ounces) plus 1
  package (3 ounces) cream
  cheese, softened
⅓ cup sugar

¼ cup butter or margarine,
  softened
1½ teaspoons vanilla
1 cup heavy or whipping cream
Peach Topping
Grated chocolate (optional)

Prepare Crumb-Nut Crust; set aside. Melt chocolate chips in top of double boiler over hot, not boiling, water, stirring until smooth. Combine cream cheese and sugar in large mixer bowl; add butter, beating until smooth. Blend in vanilla. Beat in melted chocolate all at once. Whip cream until stiff; fold into chocolate mixture.

Spoon into prepared crust; chill while preparing Peach Topping. Spoon topping onto chocolate layer and chill thoroughly. Garnish with grated chocolate.

10 to 12 servings

CRUMB-NUT CRUST

5 ounces almonds or pecans
¾ cup vanilla wafer crumbs
  (about 25 wafers)

¼ cup confectioners' sugar
¼ cup butter or margarine,
  melted

If using almonds, toast in shallow baking pan at 350° for 8 to 10 minutes, stirring frequently; cool. Chop nuts very finely in food processor or blender (you should have 1 cup). Combine nuts with wafer crumbs and confectioners' sugar in medium bowl; drizzle with melted butter. Press onto bottom and 1½ inches up side of 9-inch springform pan.

Note: You may substitute 1¾ cups graham cracker crumbs for the nuts and vanilla wafer crumbs.

PEACH TOPPING

1 teaspoon unflavored gelatine
1 tablespoon cold water
2 tablespoons boiling water
1 cup heavy or whipping cream

2 tablespoons sugar
1 teaspoon vanilla
½ cup sweetened peaches,
  drained and diced

Sprinkle gelatine onto cold water in small glass dish; allow to stand a few minutes to soften. Add boiling water and stir until gelatine is dissolved. Whip cream and sugar until stiff; beat in gelatine mixture and vanilla. Fold in diced peaches.

Top: No-Bake Chocolate Cheesecake
Bottom: Strawberry Chocolate Chip Cheesecake (see page 20)

STRAWBERRY CHOCOLATE CHIP CHEESECAKE

Pastry Crust
3 packages (8 ounces each) cream cheese, softened
3/4 cup sugar
1 package (10 ounces) frozen sliced strawberries with syrup, thawed
2/3 cup unsifted all-purpose flour

3 eggs
1 teaspoon strawberry extract
4 or 5 drops red food color
1 cup HERSHEY'S MINI CHIPS Semi-Sweet Chocolate
Sweetened whipped cream (optional)
Fresh strawberries (optional)

Prepare Pastry Crust; set aside. Beat cream cheese and sugar in large mixer bowl until smooth. Puree strawberries with syrup in food processor or blender; add to cream cheese mixture. Blend in flour, eggs, strawberry extract and food color. Stir in MINI CHIPS Chocolates.

Pour into prepared crust. Bake at 450° for 10 minutes; without opening oven door, decrease temperature to 250° and continue to bake for 50 to 60 minutes or until set. Cool; loosen cake from side of pan. Cover; chill several hours or overnight. Serve topped with sweetened whipped cream and strawberries.

10 to 12 servings

PASTRY CRUST

1/3 cup butter or margarine, softened
1/3 cup sugar

1 egg
1 1/4 cups unsifted all-purpose flour

Cream butter and sugar in small mixer bowl; blend in egg. Add flour; mix well. Spread dough on bottom and 1 1/2 inches up side of 9-inch springform pan. Bake at 450° for 5 minutes; cool.

LICKETY-SPLIT COCOA CAKE

1 1/2 cups unsifted all-purpose flour
1 cup sugar
1/4 cup HERSHEY'S Cocoa
1 teaspoon baking soda
1/2 teaspoon salt

1 cup water
1/4 cup plus 2 tablespoons vegetable oil
1 tablespoon vinegar
1 teaspoon vanilla

Combine flour, sugar, cocoa, baking soda and salt in large bowl. Add water, oil, vinegar and vanilla; stir with spoon or wire whisk just until batter is smooth and ingredients are well blended.

Pour into greased and floured 9-inch layer pan or 8-inch square pan. Bake at 350° for 35 to 40 minutes or until cake tester comes out clean. Cool in pan; frost as desired (see pages 88–93).

6 to 8 servings

CHOCOLATE-STRAWBERRY CHIFFON SQUARES

1½ cups unsifted cake flour
1 cup sugar
½ cup HERSHEY'S Cocoa
¾ teaspoon baking soda
½ teaspoon salt
1 cup buttermilk or sour milk*
½ cup vegetable oil
2 egg yolks
2 egg whites
½ cup sugar
Berry Cream
Fresh strawberries

Combine cake flour, 1 cup sugar, the cocoa, baking soda and salt in large mixer bowl. Add buttermilk, oil and egg yolks; beat until smooth. Beat egg whites in small mixer bowl until foamy; gradually add ½ cup sugar, beating until very stiff peaks form. Gently fold egg whites into chocolate batter. Pour into greased and floured 13×9-inch pan. Bake at 350° for 30 to 35 minutes or until cake springs back when touched lightly in center. Cool in pan on wire rack. Just before serving, prepare Berry Cream; frost top of cake. Cut into squares and garnish with strawberries. Refrigerate leftovers.

10 to 12 servings

*To sour milk: Use 1 tablespoon vinegar plus milk to equal 1 cup.

BERRY CREAM

1 cup sweetened sliced
   strawberries
1 cup heavy or whipping cream
1 teaspoon vanilla
2 or 3 drops red food color
   (optional)

Mash or puree strawberries in blender or food processor (you should have ½ cup). Whip cream until stiff; gently fold in puree, vanilla and food color.

Chocolate-Strawberry Chiffon Squares

Chocolate Ricotta Cheesecake

CHOCOLATE RICOTTA CHEESECAKE

Graham Crust
3 cups ricotta or low-fat cottage
  cheese
1 cup sugar
4 eggs
1 cup heavy or whipping cream
¹/₃ cup HERSHEY'S Cocoa

¹/₄ cup unsifted all-purpose flour
¹/₈ teaspoon salt
¹/₂ teaspoon vanilla
Glazed Fruit
Sweetened whipped cream
  (optional)

Prepare Graham Crust; set aside. Place ricotta cheese, sugar and eggs in food processor or blender container; process until smooth. Add cream, cocoa, flour, salt and vanilla; process until smooth.

Pour into prepared crust. Bake at 350° about 1 hour and 15 minutes or until set. Turn off oven; open door and let cheesecake remain in oven 1 hour. Cool completely; chill thoroughly. Just before serving, arrange Glazed Fruit on top of cheesecake. With pastry tube, make a border of sweetened whipped cream around edge.   *10 to 12 servings*

(continued)

GRAHAM CRUST

1 cup graham cracker crumbs
2 tablespoons sugar

¼ cup butter or margarine, melted

Combine graham cracker crumbs, sugar and melted butter. Press mixture onto bottom and ½ inch up side of 9–inch springform pan. Bake at 350° for 8 to 10 minutes; cool.

GLAZED FRUIT

½ cup sliced nectarines*
½ cup blueberries*

¼ cup apricot preserves

Stir together fruit and preserves until fruit pieces are well coated.

*You may substitute peaches, pitted sweet cherries, strawberries or canned pineapple chunks for the nectarines and blueberries.

PARTY CHOCOLATE CHEESECAKE CUPS

Graham Shells
2 packages (8 ounces each) cream cheese, softened
1 cup sour cream
1¼ cups sugar
⅓ cup HERSHEY'S Cocoa
2 tablespoons flour

3 eggs
1 teaspoon vanilla
1 cup sour cream
2 tablespoons sugar
1 teaspoon vanilla
Cherry pie filling

Prepare Graham Shells; set aside. Combine cream cheese and sour cream in large mixer bowl. Combine sugar, cocoa and flour; add to cream cheese mixture, blending well. Add eggs, one at a time, beating well after each addition. Blend in 1 teaspoon vanilla.

Fill each prepared cup almost full with cheese mixture (mixture rises only slightly during baking). Bake at 350° for 15 to 20 minutes. Turn off oven; let cheese cups remain in oven 45 minutes without opening door. Combine sour cream, sugar and 1 teaspoon vanilla; stir until sugar is dissolved. Spread heaping teaspoonful sour cream mixture on each cup. Cool completely; chill thoroughly. Garnish with dollop of cherry pie filling just before serving.

2 dozen desserts

GRAHAM SHELLS

1½ cups graham cracker crumbs
⅓ cup sugar

¼ cup butter or margarine, melted

Line 24 muffin cups (2½ inches in diameter) with paper baking cups. Combine graham cracker crumbs, sugar and melted butter. Press about 1 tablespoon onto bottom of each cup.

MARBLE CHIFFON CAKE

⅓ cup HERSHEY'S Cocoa
2 tablespoons sugar
¼ cup water
2 tablespoons vegetable oil
2 cups unsifted all-purpose flour
1½ cups sugar
3 teaspoons baking powder
1 teaspoon salt

½ cup vegetable oil
7 egg yolks, at room temperature
¾ cup cold water
2 teaspoons vanilla
7 egg whites, at room temperature
½ teaspoon cream of tartar
Cocoa Glaze

Combine cocoa, 2 tablespoons sugar, ¼ cup water and 2 tablespoons oil in small bowl until smooth; set aside. Combine flour, 1½ cups sugar, the baking powder and salt in large mixer bowl; add ½ cup oil, the egg yolks, ¾ cup cold water and the vanilla. Beat on low speed until combined. Beat 5 minutes on high speed. With clean beaters, beat egg whites and cream of tartar in another large mixer bowl until stiff peaks form.

Pour batter in thin stream over entire surface of egg whites; fold in lightly, using rubber spatula. Remove one-third of the batter to another bowl; gently fold in chocolate mixture. Pour half the vanilla batter into ungreased 10-inch tube pan; spread half the chocolate batter over vanilla. Repeat layers; gently swirl with spatula or knife for marbled effect. Bake at 325° for 65 to 70 minutes or until cake springs back when touched lightly: Invert cake over heat-proof funnel or bottle until completely cool. Loosen cake from pan; invert onto serving plate. Spread top with Cocoa Glaze.   *12 to 16 servings*

COCOA GLAZE

2 tablespoons butter or
margarine
¼ cup HERSHEY'S Cocoa

3 tablespoons water
½ teaspoon vanilla
1¼ cups confectioners' sugar

Melt butter in small saucepan over low heat. Stir in cocoa and water. Cook, stirring constantly, until mixture thickens; *do not boil*. Remove from heat. Stir in vanilla. Gradually add confectioners' sugar; beat with wire whisk until smooth.

Top: Mousse-Filled Cocoa Chiffon Cake (see page 26)
Bottom: Marble Chiffon Cake

MOUSSE-FILLED COCOA CHIFFON CAKE

1¾ cups sugar
1½ cups unsifted cake flour
⅔ cup HERSHEY'S Cocoa
2 teaspoons baking powder
1 teaspoon salt
½ teaspoon baking soda
½ cup vegetable oil
7 egg yolks

¾ cup cold water
2 teaspoons vanilla
7 egg whites, at room
  temperature
½ teaspoon cream of tartar
¼ cup sugar
  Mousse Filling
  Chocolate Cream Frosting

Combine 1¾ cups sugar, the cake flour, cocoa, baking powder, salt and baking soda in large mixing bowl. Make a "well" in mixture and add in order: oil,
egg yolks, water and vanilla. Beat until smooth. Beat egg whites and cream of
tartar in large mixing bowl until foamy. Gradually add ¼ cup sugar and beat
until stiff peaks form. Gradually pour chocolate batter over beaten egg whites,
gently folding just until blended. Pour into ungreased 10-inch tube pan. Bake
at 325° for 1 hour and 20 minutes or until cake springs back when touched
lightly. Meanwhile, prepare Mousse Filling and Chocolate Cream Frosting.

Invert cake over heat-proof funnel or bottle until completely cool. Loosen cake
from pan; invert onto serving plate. Slice ¾-inch-thick layer from top of cake;
set aside. Being careful to leave 1-inch-thick walls and base, cut a neat cavity in
cake. With fork, remove section of cake between the cuts. Spoon Mousse Filling into cavity. Replace top of cake; press gently. Frost cake with Chocolate
Cream Frosting. Chill several hours. Refrigerate leftovers.   *12 to 16 servings*

MOUSSE FILLING

1 envelope unflavored gelatine
2 tablespoons cold water
⅓ cup water
⅓ cup HERSHEY'S Cocoa

⅔ cup sugar
1½ cups heavy or whipping cream
2 teaspoons vanilla

Sprinkle gelatine onto 2 tablespoons water in small glass dish; set aside to
soften. Bring ⅓ cup water to boil in small saucepan; stir in cocoa over low heat
until smooth and thickened. Add softened gelatine, stirring until dissolved.
Remove from heat; stir in sugar. Cool to room temperature. Whip cream with
vanilla until stiff peaks form. Gradually add chocolate mixture while beating
on low speed just until well blended. Chill 30 minutes.

CHOCOLATE CREAM FROSTING

¾ cup confectioners' sugar
6 tablespoons HERSHEY'S Cocoa

1½ cups heavy or whipping cream
¾ teaspoon vanilla

Combine confectioners' sugar and cocoa in small mixer bowl. Add cream and
vanilla; beat until stiff. Cover; chill.

Marble Cheesecake

MARBLE CHEESECAKE

Graham Crust (page 23)
3 packages (8 ounces each) cream
    cheese, softened
3/4 cup sugar
1/2 cup sour cream
2 teaspoons vanilla

3 tablespoons flour
3 eggs
1/4 cup HERSHEY'S Cocoa
1/4 cup sugar
1 tablespoon vegetable oil
1/2 teaspoon vanilla

Prepare Graham Crust; set aside. Combine cream cheese, 3/4 cup sugar, the sour cream and 2 teaspoons vanilla in large mixer bowl; beat on medium speed until smooth. Add flour, 1 tablespoon at a time, blending well. Add eggs; beat well. Combine cocoa and 1/4 cup sugar in small bowl. Add oil, 1/2 teaspoon vanilla and 1 1/2 cups of the cream cheese mixture; mix until well blended.

Spoon plain and chocolate mixtures alternately into prepared crust, ending with dollops of chocolate on top; gently swirl with knife or spatula for marbled effect. Bake at 450° for 10 minutes; without opening oven door, decrease temperature to 250° and continue to bake for 30 minutes. Turn off oven; let cheesecake remain in oven 30 minutes without opening door. Remove from oven; loosen cake from side of pan. Cool completely; chill thoroughly.

10 to 12 servings

Center top: Creme-Filled Cupcakes. Left to right: Chocolatetown Cupcakes with Chocolate Buttercream Frosting (see page 92) and Chocolate-Coconut Frosting (see page 88).

CREME-FILLED CUPCAKES

³/₄ cup shortening	¹/₂ cup HERSHEY'S Cocoa
1¹/₄ cups sugar	1 teaspoon baking soda
2 eggs	¹/₂ teaspoon salt
1 teaspoon vanilla	1 cup milk
1³/₄ cups unsifted all-purpose flour	Vanilla Creme

Cream shortening and sugar in large mixer bowl. Add eggs and vanilla; blend well. Combine flour, cocoa, baking soda and salt; add alternately with milk to creamed mixture. Fill paper-lined muffin cups (2¹/₂ inches in diameter) two-thirds full with batter. Bake at 375° for 20 to 25 minutes or until cake tester comes out clean. Cool completely.

Prepare Vanilla Creme; spoon into pastry bag with open star tip. Insert tip into center of top of cupcake; gently squeeze until cupcake begins to peak. Cover top with swirl of filling. (Or cut a 1¹/₂-inch cone from top of cupcake. Fill; replace cone. Swirl filling over top.)   *About 2 dozen cupcakes*

VANILLA CREME

¹/₄ cup unsifted all-purpose flour	¹/₄ cup shortening
¹/₂ cup milk	2 teaspoons vanilla
¹/₄ cup butter or margarine,	¹/₄ teaspoon salt
softened	4 cups confectioners' sugar

Combine flour and milk in small saucepan; cook over low heat, stirring constantly with wire whisk, until mixture thickens and just begins to boil. Remove from heat; chill. Cream butter and shortening in large mixer bowl; blend in vanilla, salt and the chilled flour mixture. Gradually add confectioners' sugar; beat to spreading consistency.

CHOCOLATETOWN CUPCAKES

¹/₂ cup butter or margarine,
softened
1 cup sugar
1 teaspoon vanilla
4 eggs

1¹/₄ cups unsifted all-purpose flour
³/₄ teaspoon baking soda
1¹/₂ cups (16-ounce can)
HERSHEY'S Syrup

Cream butter, sugar and vanilla in large mixer bowl until light and fluffy. Add eggs; beat well. Combine flour and baking soda; add alternately with syrup to creamed mixture. Fill paper-lined muffin cups (2¹/₂ inches in diameter) half full with batter. Bake at 375° for 15 to 20 minutes or until cake tester comes out clean. Cool; frost as desired (see pages 88–93).

About 2¹/₂ dozen cupcakes

COCOA MEDALLION CAKE

³/₄ cup HERSHEY'S Cocoa
³/₄ cup boiling water
¹/₄ cup butter or margarine,
softened
¹/₄ cup shortening
2 cups sugar

1 teaspoon vanilla
¹/₈ teaspoon salt
2 eggs
1¹/₂ teaspoons baking soda
1 cup buttermilk or sour milk*
1³/₄ cups unsifted all-purpose flour

Stir together cocoa and boiling water until smooth; set aside. Cream butter, shortening, sugar, vanilla and salt in large mixer bowl until light and fluffy. Add eggs; beat well. Stir baking soda into buttermilk; add alternately with flour to creamed mixture. Blend in cocoa mixture.

Pour into two greased and wax paper-lined 9-inch layer pans or 8-inch square pans. Bake at 350° for 30 to 35 minutes for 9-inch pans or 40 to 45 minutes for 8-inch pans, or until cake tester comes out clean. Cool 10 minutes; remove from pans. Cool completely; frost as desired (see pages 88–93).

8 to 10 servings

*To sour milk: Use 1 tablespoon vinegar plus milk to equal 1 cup.

VARIATION
Picnic Medallion Cake: Prepare batter as directed above; pour into greased and floured 13 × 9-inch pan. Bake at 350° for 40 to 45 minutes or until cake tester comes out clean. Cool completely; frost as desired.

ORANGE COCOA CAKE

$^1/_2$ cup HERSHEY'S Cocoa
$^1/_2$ cup boiling water
$^1/_4$ cup butter or margarine,
    softened
$^1/_4$ cup shortening
2 cups sugar
$^1/_8$ teaspoon salt
1 teaspoon vanilla
2 eggs

$1^1/_2$ teaspoons baking soda
1 cup buttermilk or sour milk*
$1^3/_4$ cups unsifted all-purpose flour
3 tablespoons buttermilk or sour
    milk*
$^1/_8$ teaspoon baking soda
$^3/_4$ teaspoon grated orange peel
$^1/_4$ teaspoon orange extract
Orange Buttercream Frosting

Grease three 8- or 9-inch layer pans and line with wax paper; set aside. Stir together cocoa and boiling water in small bowl until smooth; set aside. Cream butter, shortening, sugar, salt and vanilla in large mixer bowl until light and fluffy. Add eggs; beat well. Stir $1^1/_2$ teaspoons baking soda into 1 cup buttermilk; add alternately with flour to creamed mixture.

Measure $1^2/_3$ cups batter into small bowl. Stir in 3 tablespoons buttermilk, $^1/_8$ teaspoon baking soda, the orange peel and orange extract; pour into one prepared pan. Blend cocoa mixture into remaining batter; divide evenly among remaining two prepared pans. Bake at 350° for 25 to 30 minutes or until cake tester comes out clean. Cool 10 minutes; remove from pans. Cool completely. Place one chocolate layer on serving plate; spread with some of the Orange Buttercream Frosting. Top with orange layer and spread with frosting. Top with remaining chocolate layer and frost entire cake.

10 to 12 servings

*To sour milk: Use 1 tablespoon vinegar plus milk to equal 1 cup; use $^1/_2$ teaspoon vinegar plus milk to equal 3 tablespoons.

ORANGE BUTTERCREAM FROSTING

$^2/_3$ cup butter or margarine,
    softened
6 cups confectioners' sugar

2 teaspoons grated orange peel
$1^1/_2$ teaspoons vanilla
4 to 6 tablespoons milk

Cream butter, 1 cup confectioners' sugar, the orange peel and vanilla in large mixer bowl. Add remaining confectioners' sugar alternately with milk, beating to spreading consistency.

Orange Cocoa Cake

CHOCOLATE PEANUT BUTTER MARBLE CAKE

¼ cup HERSHEY'S Cocoa
2 tablespoons confectioners'
  sugar
2 tablespoons butter or
  margarine, softened
2 tablespoons hot water
1 cup REESE'S Peanut Butter
  Chips

1 tablespoon shortening
1 package (18½ ounces) white
  cake mix (pudding-in-the-
  mix type)
½ cup packed light brown sugar
1¼ cups water
3 eggs

Combine cocoa, confectioners' sugar, butter and 2 tablespoons hot water in small bowl until smooth; set aside. Melt peanut butter chips and shortening in top of double boiler over hot, not boiling, water; set aside. Combine dry cake mix, brown sugar, 1¼ cups water, the eggs and melted peanut butter mixture in large mixer bowl; beat on low speed until moistened. Beat 2 minutes on medium speed until smooth. Add 1½ cups batter to reserved cocoa mixture; blend well. Pour remaining batter into greased and floured 13×9-inch pan; spoon dollops of chocolate batter on top. Swirl with knife or spatula for marbled effect. Bake at 350° for 40 to 45 minutes or until cake tester comes out clean. Cool; frost as desired (see pages 88–93).   *10 to 12 servings*

COCOA CHEESECAKE

Graham Crust
2 packages (8 ounces each) cream
  cheese, softened
¾ cup sugar
½ cup HERSHEY'S Cocoa

1 teaspoon vanilla
2 eggs
1 cup sour cream
2 tablespoons sugar
1 teaspoon vanilla

Prepare Graham Crust; set aside. Beat cream cheese, ¾ cup sugar, the cocoa and 1 teaspoon vanilla in large mixer bowl until light and fluffy. Add eggs; blend well. Pour into prepared crust. Bake at 375° for 20 minutes. Remove cheesecake from oven; cool for 15 minutes.

Combine sour cream, 2 tablespoons sugar and 1 teaspoon vanilla; stir until smooth. Spread evenly over baked filling. Bake at 425° for 10 minutes. Cool; chill several hours or overnight.   *10 to 12 servings*

GRAHAM CRUST

1½ cups graham cracker crumbs
  ⅓ cup sugar

⅓ cup butter or margarine,
  melted

Combine graham cracker crumbs, sugar and melted butter. Press mixture onto bottom and halfway up side of 9-inch springform pan.

Fudgey Pecan Cake

FUDGEY PECAN CAKE

³/₄ cup butter or margarine,
   melted
1¹/₂ cups sugar
1¹/₂ teaspoons vanilla
   3 egg yolks
¹/₂ cup plus 1 tablespoon
   HERSHEY'S Cocoa
¹/₂ cup unsifted all-purpose flour
   3 tablespoons vegetable oil

3 tablespoons water
³/₄ cup finely chopped pecans
3 egg whites, at room
   temperature
¹/₈ teaspoon cream of tartar
¹/₈ teaspoon salt
   Royal Glaze (page 88)
   Pecan halves (optional)

Line bottom of 9-inch springform pan with aluminum foil; butter foil and side of pan. Set aside. Combine ³/₄ cup melted butter, the sugar and vanilla in large mixer bowl; beat well. Add egg yolks, one at a time, beating well after each addition. Blend in cocoa, flour, oil and water; beat well. Stir in chopped pecans. Beat egg whites, cream of tartar and salt in small mixer bowl until stiff peaks form. Carefully fold into chocolate mixture. Pour into prepared pan. Bake at 350° for 45 minutes or until top begins to crack slightly. (Cake will not test done in center.) Cool 1 hour. Cover; chill until firm. Remove side of pan.

Prepare Royal Glaze. Pour over cake, allowing glaze to run down side. With narrow metal spatula, spread glaze evenly on top and side. Allow to harden. Garnish with pecan halves.   *10 to 12 servings*

Chocolate Swirl Cake

CHOCOLATE SWIRL CAKE

1 cup butter or margarine, softened
2 cups sugar
2 teaspoons vanilla
3 eggs
2³/₄ cups unsifted all-purpose flour
1 teaspoon baking soda
¹/₂ teaspoon salt
1 cup buttermilk or sour milk*
1 cup HERSHEY'S Syrup
¹/₄ teaspoon baking soda
1 cup flaked coconut (optional)

Cream butter, sugar and vanilla in large mixer bowl until light and fluffy. Add eggs; beat well. Combine flour, 1 teaspoon baking soda and the salt; add alternately with buttermilk to creamed mixture. Combine syrup and ¹/₄ teaspoon baking soda. Measure 2 cups batter into small bowl; blend in syrup mixture.

Add coconut to remaining batter; pour into greased and floured 12-cup Bundt pan or 10-inch tube pan. Pour chocolate batter over vanilla batter in pan; *do not mix.* Bake at 350° about 70 minutes or until cake tester comes out clean. Cool 15 minutes; remove from pan. Cool completely; glaze or frost as desired (see pages 88–93). *12 to 16 servings*

*To sour milk: Use 1 tablespoon vinegar plus milk to equal 1 cup.

Pies
& Pastries

CLASSIC CHOCOLATE CREAM PIE

9-inch pastry shell or crumb crust
2½ blocks (2½ ounces) HERSHEY'S Unsweetened Baking Chocolate, broken into pieces
2 cups milk
1⅓ cups sugar
3 tablespoons flour
3 tablespoons cornstarch
½ teaspoon salt
3 egg yolks
1 cup milk
2 tablespoons butter or margarine
1½ teaspoons vanilla
3 egg whites, at room temperature
¼ teaspoon cream of tartar
6 tablespoons sugar

Bake pastry shell; set aside. Melt baking chocolate pieces with 2 cups milk in medium saucepan over medium heat, stirring constantly. Cook and stir *just* until mixture boils; remove from heat. Combine 1⅓ cups sugar, the flour, cornstarch and salt in small bowl. Blend egg yolks with 1 cup milk; add to dry ingredients. Blend into chocolate mixture in saucepan. Cook over medium heat, stirring constantly, until mixture boils; boil and stir 1 minute. Remove from heat; blend in butter and vanilla. Pour into cooled shell.

Beat egg whites and cream of tartar in small mixer bowl until foamy. Gradually add 6 tablespoons sugar; beat until stiff peaks form. Spread meringue onto hot pie filling, carefully sealing meringue to edge of crust. Bake in preheated 350° oven for 8 to 10 minutes or until lightly browned. Cool to room temperature; chill several hours or overnight. *8 servings*

VARIATION
Chocolate Rum Cream Pie: Substitute 3 to 4 tablespoons rum for the vanilla.

BRANDY ALEXANDER PIE

Chocolate Petal Crust
30 large marshmallows
1/2 cup milk
1 cup HERSHEY'S Semi-Sweet
    Chocolate Chips

1 teaspoon vanilla
1 to 2 tablespoons brandy
1 to 2 tablespoons crème de
    cacao
2 cups heavy or whipping cream

Prepare Chocolate Petal Crust; set aside. Combine marshmallows and milk in medium saucepan; cook over low heat, stirring constantly, until marshmallows are melted and mixture is smooth. Pour half the marshmallow mixture into small bowl; set aside. Add chocolate chips to the remaining marshmallow mixture; return to low heat and stir until chips are melted. Remove from heat and stir in vanilla; cool to room temperature. Stir brandy and crème de cacao into reserved marshmallow mixture in small bowl; chill until mixture mounds slightly when dropped from a spoon.

Whip cream until stiff. Fold 2 cups of the whipped cream into cooled chocolate mixture; spoon into cooled crust. Blend remaining whipped cream into chilled brandy mixture; spread over chocolate mixture. Chill about 2 hours or until firm. Garnish as desired.   *8 servings*

CHOCOLATE PETAL CRUST

1/2 cup butter or margarine,
    softened
1 cup sugar
1 egg
1 teaspoon vanilla

1 1/4 cups unsifted all-purpose flour
1/2 cup HERSHEY'S Cocoa
3/4 teaspoon baking soda
1/4 teaspoon salt

Cream butter, sugar, egg and vanilla in large mixer bowl. Combine flour, cocoa, baking soda and salt; stir into creamed mixture. Shape soft dough into two rolls, 1 1/2 inches in diameter each. Wrap in plastic wrap; chill several hours. Cut one roll into 1/8-inch slices; arrange slices, edges touching, on bottom, up side and onto rim of greased 9-inch pie pan. (Small spaces in crust will not affect pie.) Bake at 375° for 8 to 10 minutes. Cool.

Enough dough for 2 crusts

Note: Remaining roll of dough may be frozen for later use. Or, bake as chocolate refrigerator cookies. Cut roll into 1/8-inch slices. Place on ungreased cookie sheet. Bake at 375° for 8 to 10 minutes or until almost set. Cool slightly. Remove from cookie sheet; cool completely on wire rack. Makes about 1 1/2 dozen cookies.

Top: Brandy Alexander Pie
Bottom: Black Bottom Pie (see page 38)

BLACK BOTTOM PIE

9-inch pastry shell or crumb
   crust
1/2 cup sugar
1/3 cup HERSHEY'S Cocoa
1/4 cup butter or margarine,
   softened
1 envelope unflavored gelatine
1/4 cup cold water
2 cups milk

4 egg yolks
1/2 cup sugar
1/4 cup cornstarch
1 teaspoon vanilla
2 tablespoons rum
4 egg whites
1/2 cup sugar
Grated chocolate

Bake pastry shell; set aside. Combine 1/2 cup sugar, the cocoa and butter in medium bowl; set aside. Sprinkle gelatine onto cold water in small bowl; let stand 1 minute to soften. Place bowl in pan of simmering water to dissolve gelatine. Combine milk, egg yolks, 1/2 cup sugar and the cornstarch in medium saucepan. Cook over medium heat, stirring constantly, until mixture boils; boil and stir 1 minute. Remove from heat; measure 1 1/2 cups of the custard and blend into cocoa-sugar mixture. Add vanilla and pour into cooled shell; chill until set.

Combine dissolved gelatine with remaining custard; add rum and set aside. Beat egg whites in small mixer bowl until foamy; gradually add 1/2 cup sugar and beat until stiff peaks form. Fold egg whites into gelatine-custard mixture. Chill 15 minutes or until partially set. Spoon over chocolate custard in crust. Chill until set. Garnish with grated chocolate. *8 servings*

EASY CHOCOLATE MOUSSE PIE

Graham Cracker Crust
1 package (8 ounces) cream
   cheese, softened
1/2 cup HERSHEY'S Cocoa

1 cup confectioners' sugar
1 1/2 teaspoons vanilla
2 cups heavy or whipping cream

Prepare Graham Cracker Crust; set aside. Beat cream cheese and cocoa in large mixer bowl until fluffy and well blended. Gradually add confectioners' sugar; blend well. Stir in vanilla. Whip cream until stiff; fold into cheese mixture. Pour into cooled crust; chill until firm. Garnish as desired.

8 servings

GRAHAM CRACKER CRUST

1 1/2 cups graham cracker crumbs
1/3 cup butter or margarine, melted

3 tablespoons sugar

Combine graham cracker crumbs, melted butter and sugar in small bowl. Press mixture firmly onto bottom and up side of 9-inch pie pan. Bake at 350° for 10 minutes; cool.

Chocolate Banana Cream Pie

CHOCOLATE BANANA CREAM PIE

9-inch pastry shell or crumb
   crust
1¼ cups sugar
  ⅓ cup HERSHEY'S Cocoa
  ⅓ cup cornstarch
  ¼ teaspoon salt
  3 cups milk

3 tablespoons butter or
  margarine
1½ teaspoons vanilla
2 medium bananas, sliced
  Sweetened whipped cream
  Additional banana slices
  (optional)

Bake pastry shell; set aside. Combine sugar, cocoa, cornstarch and salt in medium saucepan; gradually add milk, stirring until smooth. Cook over medium
heat, stirring constantly, until mixture boils; boil and stir 3 minutes. Remove
from heat; blend in butter and vanilla. Pour into bowl; press plastic wrap directly onto surface. Cool to room temperature.

Cover bottom of cooled shell with small amount of filling. Arrange banana
slices over filling; cover with remaining filling. Chill 3 to 4 hours or until firm.
Garnish with sweetened whipped cream and banana slices.

8 servings

Top: Chocolate-Filled Cream Puffs. Middle: Chocolate-Almond Tarts.
Bottom: Napoleons (see page 42).

CHOCOLATE-FILLED CREAM PUFFS

1 cup water
¹/₂ cup butter or margarine
¹/₄ teaspoon salt
1 cup unsifted all-purpose flour

4 eggs
Chocolate Cream Filling
Confectioners' sugar

Heat water, butter and salt to rolling boil in medium saucepan. Add flour all at once; stir vigorously over low heat about 1 minute or until mixture leaves side of pan and forms a ball. Remove from heat; add eggs, one at a time, beating well after each addition until smooth and velvety.

Drop by scant ¹/₄ cupfuls onto ungreased cookie sheet. Bake at 400° for 35 to 40 minutes or until puffed and golden brown. While puff is warm, horizontally slice off small portion of top; reserve tops. Remove any soft filaments of dough; cool puffs. Prepare Chocolate Cream Filling; fill puffs. Replace tops; dust with confectioners' sugar. Chill. *About 12 cream puffs*
(continued)

CHOCOLATE CREAM FILLING

1¹/₄ cups sugar
¹/₃ cup HERSHEY'S Cocoa
¹/₃ cup cornstarch
¹/₄ teaspoon salt
3 cups milk

3 egg yolks, slightly beaten
2 tablespoons butter or
   margarine
1¹/₂ teaspoons vanilla

Combine sugar, cocoa, cornstarch and salt in medium saucepan; stir in milk. Cook over medium heat, stirring constantly, until mixture boils; boil and stir 1 minute. Remove from heat. Gradually stir small amount of chocolate mixture into egg yolks; blend well. Return egg mixture to chocolate mixture in pan; stir and heat just until boiling. Remove from heat; blend in butter and vanilla. Pour into bowl; press plastic wrap directly onto surface. Cool.

VARIATION
Miniature Cream Puffs: Drop dough by level teaspoonfuls onto ungreased cookie sheet. Bake at 400° for about 15 minutes. Fill as directed above.

About 8 dozen miniature cream puffs

CHOCOLATE-ALMOND TARTS

Chocolate Tart Shells
³/₄ cup sugar
¹/₄ cup HERSHEY'S Cocoa
2 tablespoons cornstarch
2 tablespoons flour
¹/₄ teaspoon salt

2 cups milk
2 egg yolks, slightly beaten
2 tablespoons butter or
   margarine
¹/₄ teaspoon almond extract
Sliced almonds

Prepare Chocolate Tart Shells; set aside. Combine sugar, cocoa, cornstarch, flour and salt in medium saucepan; blend in milk and egg yolks. Cook over medium heat, stirring constantly, until mixture boils; boil and stir 1 minute. Remove from heat; blend in butter and almond extract.

Pour into cooled shells; press plastic wrap directly onto surface. Chill. Garnish tops with sliced almonds.

6 tarts

CHOCOLATE TART SHELLS

1¹/₂ cups vanilla wafer crumbs
   (about 45 wafers)
¹/₃ cup confectioners' sugar

¹/₄ cup HERSHEY'S Cocoa
6 tablespoons butter or
   margarine, melted

Combine crumbs, confectioners' sugar, cocoa and melted butter in medium bowl; stir until completely blended. Divide mixture among six 4-ounce tart pans; press mixture firmly onto bottoms and up sides of pans. Bake at 350° for 5 minutes. Cool.

NAPOLEONS

2 sheets (17¼-ounce package)
frozen puff pastry
Chocolate Cream Filling

Vanilla Frosting
Chocolate Glaze

Thaw folded pastry sheets as directed; gently unfold. Roll each on floured surface to 15 × 12-inch rectangle. Place on ungreased cookie sheets; prick each sheet thoroughly with fork. Bake at 350° for 18 to 22 minutes or until puffed and lightly browned. Cool completely on cookie sheets. Prepare Chocolate Cream Filling.

Cut one rectangle lengthwise into three equal pieces. Place one piece on serving plate; spread with one-fourth of the Chocolate Cream Filling. Top with second piece of pastry; spread with one-fourth of the filling. Place remaining piece on top; set aside. Repeat procedure with remaining pastry and filling.

Prepare Vanilla Frosting; spread half the frosting on each rectangle. Prepare Chocolate Glaze; drizzle half the glaze in decorative design over frosting on each rectangle. Cover; chill at least 1 hour or until filling is firm. Cut each rectangle into six pieces. *12 servings*

CHOCOLATE CREAM FILLING

½ cup sugar
3 tablespoons cornstarch
1½ cups milk
3 egg yolks, slightly beaten

¾ cup HERSHEY'S MINI CHIPS
Semi-Sweet Chocolate
½ teaspoon vanilla

Combine sugar, cornstarch and milk in medium saucepan. Cook over medium heat, stirring constantly, until mixture just begins to boil. Remove from heat. Gradually stir small amount of mixture into egg yolks; blend well. Return egg mixture to mixture in pan. Cook over medium heat, stirring constantly, 1 minute. Remove from heat; add MINI CHIPS Chocolates and vanilla, stirring until chips are melted and mixture is smooth. Press plastic wrap directly onto surface. Cool; chill thoroughly.

VANILLA FROSTING

1½ cups confectioners' sugar
1 tablespoon light corn syrup

¼ teaspoon vanilla
1 to 2 tablespoons hot water

Combine confectioners' sugar, corn syrup, vanilla and hot water in small mixer bowl; beat to spreading consistency.

CHOCOLATE GLAZE

¼ cup butter or margarine

⅓ cup HERSHEY'S Cocoa

Melt butter in small saucepan. Remove from heat; stir in cocoa until smooth. Cool slightly.

FUDGE PECAN PIE

½ cup sugar
⅓ cup HERSHEY'S Cocoa
⅓ cup unsifted all-purpose flour
¼ teaspoon salt
1¼ cups light corn syrup
3 eggs

3 tablespoons butter or
   margarine, melted
1½ teaspoons vanilla
½ cup chopped pecans
9-inch unbaked pastry shell
Pecan halves

Combine sugar, cocoa, flour, salt, corn syrup, eggs, melted butter and vanilla in large mixer bowl; beat 30 seconds on medium speed *(do not overbeat)*. Stir in chopped pecans.

Pour into unbaked pastry shell. Bake at 350° for 55 to 60 minutes; immediately arrange pecan halves on top. Cool. (For fullest flavor, cover and let stand one day before serving.)   *8 servings*

VARIATION
Fudge Walnut Pie: Substitute dark corn syrup for light corn syrup, 1 tablespoon imitation maple flavor for vanilla and chopped walnuts and walnut halves for chopped pecans and pecan halves. Prepare and bake as directed above.

Fudge Pecan Pie

Strawberry Chocolate Pie

STRAWBERRY CHOCOLATE PIE

Cocoa Crumb Crust
3/4 cup HERSHEY'S Syrup
1/2 cup sweetened condensed
   milk*
1 egg yolk, beaten
1 teaspoon vanilla

1 cup heavy or whipping
   cream**
1 egg white
1 tablespoon sugar
Strawberry Topping

Prepare Cocoa Crumb Crust; set aside. Combine syrup, sweetened condensed milk and egg yolk in small heavy saucepan. Cook over medium heat, stirring constantly, until mixture boils. Remove from heat; stir in vanilla. Cool; chill thoroughly. Whip cream until stiff; fold into chocolate mixture. Beat egg white in small mixer bowl until foamy; add sugar and beat until stiff peaks form. Fold into chocolate cream mixture. Pour into prepared crust. Cover; freeze until firm.

Prepare Strawberry Topping; spoon onto frozen chocolate filling. Cover; freeze until serving time. Garnish as desired. *8 servings*

*Do not use evaporated milk.

**Do not use non-dairy whipped topping.

(continued)

COCOA CRUMB CRUST

1¹/₂ cups vanilla wafer crumbs
   (about 45 wafers)
¹/₃ cup HERSHEY'S Cocoa

¹/₃ cup confectioners' sugar
6 tablespoons butter or
   margarine, melted

Combine crumbs, cocoa and confectioners' sugar in medium bowl; gradually add melted butter, stirring to completely coat crumb mixture. Press mixture firmly onto bottom and up side of 9-inch pie pan; freeze.

STRAWBERRY TOPPING

1 package (10 ounces) frozen
   sliced strawberries, thawed
1 cup heavy or whipping cream

2 tablespoons sugar
2 tablespoons light corn syrup

Drain strawberries; mash or puree in blender or food processor to equal ¹/₂ to ²/₃ cup. Whip cream and sugar until stiff; fold in strawberry puree and corn syrup.

FUDGE BROWNIE PIE

2 eggs
1 cup sugar
¹/₂ cup butter or margarine,
   melted
¹/₂ cup unsifted all-purpose flour
¹/₃ cup HERSHEY'S Cocoa

¹/₄ teaspoon salt
1 teaspoon vanilla
¹/₂ cup chopped nuts (optional)
Ice cream
Hot Fudge Sauce

Beat eggs in small mixer bowl; blend in sugar and melted butter. Combine flour, cocoa and salt; add to butter mixture. Stir in vanilla and nuts.

Pour into lightly greased 8-inch pie pan. Bake at 350° for 25 to 30 minutes or until almost set (pie will not test done). Cool; cut into wedges. Serve wedges topped with scoop of ice cream and drizzled with Hot Fudge Sauce.

6 to 8 servings

HOT FUDGE SAUCE

³/₄ cup sugar
¹/₂ cup HERSHEY'S Cocoa
¹/₂ cup plus 2 tablespoons
   (5-ounce can) evaporated milk

¹/₃ cup light corn syrup
¹/₃ cup butter or margarine
1 teaspoon vanilla

Combine sugar and cocoa in small saucepan; blend in evaporated milk and corn syrup. Cook over medium heat, stirring constantly, until mixture boils; boil and stir 1 minute. Remove from heat; stir in butter and vanilla. Serve warm.

About 1³/₄ cups sauce

Cookies & Bar Cookies

SCRUMPTIOUS CHOCOLATE LAYER BARS

2 cups (12-ounce package)
HERSHEY'S Semi-Sweet
Chocolate Chips
1 package (8 ounces) cream
cheese
1/2 cup plus 2 tablespoons
(5-ounce can) evaporated
milk
1 cup chopped walnuts

1/4 cup sesame seeds (optional)
1/2 teaspoon almond extract
3 cups unsifted all-purpose flour
1 1/2 cups sugar
1 teaspoon baking powder
1/2 teaspoon salt
1 cup butter or margarine
2 eggs
1/2 teaspoon almond extract

Combine chocolate chips, cream cheese and evaporated milk in medium saucepan. Cook over low heat, stirring constantly, until chips are melted and mixture is smooth. Remove from heat; stir in walnuts, sesame seeds and 1/2 teaspoon almond extract. Blend well; set aside.

Combine remaining ingredients in large mixer bowl; blend well on low speed until mixture resembles coarse crumbs. Press half the mixture in greased 13×9-inch pan; spread with chocolate mixture. Sprinkle rest of crumbs over filling. (If mixture softens and forms a stiff dough, pinch off small pieces to use as topping.) Bake at 375° for 35 to 40 minutes or until golden brown. Cool; cut into bars. *About 3 dozen bars*

Clockwise from top left: Peanut Butter Paisley Brownies (see page 48), Scrumptious Chocolate Layer Bars and Best Brownies (see page 48)

PEANUT BUTTER PAISLEY BROWNIES

1/2 cup butter or margarine,
  softened
1/4 cup peanut butter
1 cup sugar
1 cup packed light brown sugar
3 eggs

1 teaspoon vanilla
2 cups unsifted all-purpose flour
2 teaspoons baking powder
1/4 teaspoon salt
1/2 cup (5.5-ounce can)
  HERSHEY'S Syrup

Blend butter and peanut butter in large mixer bowl. Add sugar and brown sugar; beat well. Add eggs, one at a time, beating well after each addition. Blend in vanilla. Combine flour, baking powder and salt; add to peanut butter mixture.

Spread half the batter in greased 13×9-inch pan. Spoon syrup over top. Carefully spread with remaining batter. Swirl with spatula or knife for marbled effect. Bake at 350° for 35 to 40 minutes or until lightly browned. Cool; cut into squares.   *About 3 dozen brownies*

BEST BROWNIES

1/2 cup butter or margarine,
  melted
1 cup sugar
1 teaspoon vanilla
2 eggs
1/2 cup unsifted all-purpose flour

1/3 cup HERSHEY'S Cocoa
1/4 teaspoon baking powder
1/4 teaspoon salt
1/2 cup chopped nuts (optional)
Creamy Brownie Frosting

Blend butter, sugar and vanilla in large bowl. Add eggs; using a wooden spoon, beat well. Combine flour, cocoa, baking powder and salt; gradually blend into egg mixture. Stir in nuts.

Spread in greased 9-inch square pan. Bake at 350° for 20 to 25 minutes or until brownie begins to pull away from edges of pan. Cool; frost with Creamy Brownie Frosting. Cut into squares.   *About 16 brownies*

CREAMY BROWNIE FROSTING

3 tablespoons butter or
  margarine, softened
3 tablespoons HERSHEY'S Cocoa
1 tablespoon light corn syrup or
  honey

1/2 teaspoon vanilla
1 cup confectioners' sugar
1 to 2 tablespoons milk

Cream butter, cocoa, corn syrup and vanilla in small mixer bowl. Add confectioners' sugar and milk; beat to spreading consistency.

About 1 cup frosting

Macaroon Kiss Cookies

MACAROON KISS COOKIES

¹/₃ cup butter or margarine, softened	1¹/₄ cups unsifted all-purpose flour
1 package (3 ounces) cream cheese, softened	2 teaspoons baking powder
	¹/₄ teaspoon salt
³/₄ cup sugar	5 cups (14-ounce package) flaked coconut
1 egg yolk	54 HERSHEY'S KISSES
2 teaspoons almond extract	Chocolates (9-ounce
2 teaspoons orange juice	package), unwrapped

Cream butter, cream cheese and sugar in large mixer bowl until light and fluffy. Add egg yolk, almond extract and orange juice; beat well. Combine flour, baking powder and salt; gradually add to creamed mixture. Stir in 3 cups of the coconut. Cover tightly; chill 1 hour or until firm enough to handle.

Shape dough into 1-inch balls; roll in remaining coconut. Place on ungreased cookie sheet. Bake at 350° for 10 to 12 minutes or until lightly browned. Remove from oven; immediately press unwrapped KISS on top of each cookie. Cool 1 minute. Carefully remove from cookie sheet; cool completely on wire rack.   *About 4¹/₂ dozen cookies*

REESE'S CHEWY CHOCOLATE COOKIES

1¼ cups butter or margarine,
   softened
2 cups sugar
2 eggs
2 teaspoons vanilla
2 cups unsifted all-purpose flour

¾ cup HERSHEY'S Cocoa
1 teaspoon baking soda
½ teaspoon salt
2 cups (12-ounce package)
   REESE'S Peanut Butter Chips

Cream butter and sugar in large mixer bowl until light and fluffy. Add eggs and vanilla; beat well. Combine flour, cocoa, baking soda and salt; gradually blend into creamed mixture. Stir in peanut butter chips.

Drop by teaspoonfuls onto ungreased cookie sheet. Bake at 350° for 8 to 9 minutes. *Do not overbake.* (Cookies will be soft; they will puff during baking and flatten upon cooling.) Cool until set, about 1 minute. Remove from cookie sheet; cool completely on wire rack. *About 4½ dozen cookies*

HERSHEY'S GREAT AMERICAN CHOCOLATE CHIP COOKIES

1 cup butter, softened
¾ cup sugar
¾ cup packed light brown sugar
1 teaspoon vanilla
2 eggs
2¼ cups unsifted all-purpose flour

1 teaspoon baking soda
½ teaspoon salt
2 cups (12-ounce package)
   HERSHEY'S Semi-Sweet
   Chocolate Chips
1 cup chopped nuts (optional)

Cream butter, sugar, brown sugar and vanilla in large mixer bowl until light and fluffy. Add eggs; beat well. Combine flour, baking soda and salt; gradually add to creamed mixture. Beat well. Stir in chocolate chips and nuts.

Drop by teaspoonfuls onto ungreased cookie sheet. Bake at 375° for 8 to 10 minutes or until lightly browned. Cool slightly. Remove from cookie sheet; cool completely on wire rack. *About 6 dozen cookies*

VARIATION
Milk Chocolate Chip Cookies: Substitute 2 cups (11.5-ounce package) HERSHEY'S Milk Chocolate Chips for the semi-sweet chocolate chips.

Clockwise from top left: Hershey's Great American Chocolate Chip Cookies, Reese's Chewy Chocolate Cookies, Chocolate Chip Whole Wheat Cookies (see page 52) and Chocolate Cookie Sandwiches (see page 52)

CHOCOLATE COOKIE SANDWICHES

1/2 cup shortening
1 cup sugar
1 egg
1 teaspoon vanilla
1 1/2 cups unsifted all-purpose flour

1/3 cup HERSHEY'S Cocoa
1/2 teaspoon baking soda
1/2 teaspoon salt
1/4 cup milk
Creme Filling

Cream shortening, sugar, egg and vanilla in large mixer bowl until light and fluffy. Combine flour, cocoa, baking soda and salt; add alternately with milk to creamed mixture until ingredients are combined.

Drop by teaspoonfuls onto ungreased cookie sheet. Bake at 375° for 11 to 12 minutes or just until soft-set *(do not overbake)*. Cool 1 minute. Remove from cookie sheet; cool completely on wire rack. Prepare Creme Filling. Spread bottom of one cookie with about 1 tablespoon filling; cover with another cookie. Repeat with remaining cookies and filling.

About 15 filled cookies

CREME FILLING

2 tablespoons butter or
  margarine, softened
2 tablespoons shortening

1/2 cup marshmallow creme
3/4 teaspoon vanilla
2/3 cup confectioners' sugar

Cream butter and shortening in small mixer bowl; gradually beat in marshmallow creme. Blend in vanilla and confectioners' sugar; beat to spreading consistency.

CHOCOLATE CHIP WHOLE WHEAT COOKIES

3/4 cup shortening
1 1/2 cups packed light brown sugar
1 egg
1/4 cup water
1 teaspoon vanilla
1 cup unsifted whole wheat flour

1/2 teaspoon baking soda
1/2 teaspoon salt
2 cups quick-cooking oats
1 cup chopped dried apricots or
  raisins
1 cup HERSHEY'S MINI CHIPS
  Semi-Sweet Chocolate

Cream shortening and brown sugar in large mixer bowl until light and fluffy. Add egg, water and vanilla; beat well. Combine whole wheat flour, baking soda and salt; stir into creamed mixture. Stir in oats, dried apricots and MINI CHIPS Chocolates.

Drop by teaspoonfuls onto lightly greased cookie sheet; flatten slightly. Bake at 350° for 10 to 12 minutes or until golden brown. Remove from cookie sheet; cool completely on wire rack.

About 5 dozen cookies

CHOCOLATE-CHERRY SQUARES

1 cup unsifted all-purpose flour
1/3 cup butter or margarine
1/2 cup packed light brown sugar
1/2 cup chopped nuts
Filling
Red candied cherry halves

Combine flour, butter and brown sugar in large mixer bowl. Blend on low speed to form fine crumbs, about 2 to 3 minutes. Stir in nuts. Reserve 3/4 cup crumb mixture for topping; pat remaining crumbs into ungreased 9-inch square pan. Bake at 350° for 10 minutes or until lightly browned. Prepare Filling; spread over warm crust. Sprinkle with reserved crumb mixture and garnish with cherry halves. Bake at 350° for 25 minutes or until lightly browned. Cool; cut into squares. Store in refrigerator.   *About 3 dozen squares*

FILLING

1 package (8 ounces) cream
    cheese, softened
1/2 cup sugar
1/3 cup HERSHEY'S Cocoa
1/4 cup milk
1 egg
1/2 teaspoon vanilla
1/2 cup chopped red candied
    cherries

Combine cream cheese, sugar, cocoa, milk, egg and vanilla in small mixer bowl; beat until smooth. Fold in cherries.

Chocolate-Cherry Squares

HOLIDAY CHOCOLATE COOKIES

1/2 cup butter or margarine,
    softened
3/4 cup sugar
1 egg
1 teaspoon vanilla
1 1/2 cups unsifted all-purpose flour

1/3 cup HERSHEY'S Cocoa
1/2 teaspoon baking powder
1/2 teaspoon baking soda
1/4 teaspoon salt
Decorator's Frosting

Cream butter, sugar, egg and vanilla in large mixer bowl until light and fluffy. Combine remaining ingredients except Decorator's Frosting; add to creamed mixture, blending well.

Roll a small portion of dough at a time on lightly floured surface to 1/4-inch thickness. (If too soft, chill dough until firm enough to roll.) Cut with 2 1/2-inch cutter; place on ungreased cookie sheet. Bake at 325° for 5 to 7 minutes or until only a slight indentation remains when touched lightly. Cool 1 minute. Remove from cookie sheet; cool completely on wire rack. Prepare Decorator's Frosting and decorate with holiday designs or messages.

About 3 dozen cookies

DECORATOR'S FROSTING

1 1/2 cups confectioners' sugar
2 tablespoons shortening
2 tablespoons milk

1/2 teaspoon vanilla
Red, green or yellow food color

Combine all ingredients except food color in small mixer bowl; beat until smooth and of spreading consistency. Tint with drops of food color, blending well.

CHOCOLATE CHIP CHOCOLATE COOKIES

1/2 cup butter or margarine,
    softened
1 cup sugar
1 egg
1 teaspoon vanilla
1 1/2 cups unsifted all-purpose flour

1/3 cup HERSHEY'S Cocoa
1/2 teaspoon baking soda
1/2 teaspoon salt
1/4 cup milk
1 cup HERSHEY'S Semi-Sweet
    Chocolate Chips

Cream butter, sugar, egg and vanilla in large mixer bowl until light and fluffy. Combine flour, cocoa, baking soda and salt; add alternately with milk to creamed mixture, blending well. Stir in chocolate chips.

Drop by teaspoonfuls onto ungreased cookie sheet. Bake at 375° for 10 to 12 minutes or until almost set *(do not overbake)*. Cool 1 minute. Remove from cookie sheet; cool completely on wire rack.

About 3 1/2 dozen cookies

REESE'S COOKIES

1 cup shortening, *or* ³/₄ cup
   butter or margarine, softened
1 cup sugar
¹/₂ cup packed light brown sugar
1 teaspoon vanilla
2 eggs

2 cups unsifted all-purpose flour
1 teaspoon baking soda
1 cup REESE'S Peanut Butter
   Chips
1 cup HERSHEY'S Semi-Sweet
   Chocolate Chips

Cream shortening or butter, sugar, brown sugar and vanilla in large mixer bowl until light and fluffy. Add eggs; beat well. Combine flour and baking soda; add to creamed mixture. Stir in peanut butter chips and chocolate chips.

Drop by teaspoonfuls onto ungreased cookie sheet. Bake at 350° for 10 to 12 minutes or until lightly browned. Cool slightly. Remove from cookie sheet; cool completely on wire rack. *About 5 dozen cookies*

COCOA-PECAN KISS COOKIES

1 cup butter or margarine,
   softened
²/₃ cup sugar
1 teaspoon vanilla
1²/₃ cups unsifted all-purpose flour
¹/₄ cup HERSHEY'S Cocoa

1 cup finely chopped pecans
54 HERSHEY'S KISSES
   Chocolates (9-ounce
   package), unwrapped
Confectioners' sugar

Cream butter, sugar and vanilla in large mixer bowl until light and fluffy. Combine flour and cocoa; blend into creamed mixture. Add pecans; beat on low speed until well blended. Chill dough 1 hour or until firm enough to handle.

Shape scant tablespoon of dough around each unwrapped KISS, covering completely; shape into balls. Place on ungreased cookie sheet. Bake at 375° for 10 to 12 minutes or until almost set. Cool slightly. Remove from cookie sheet; cool completely on wire rack. Roll in confectioners' sugar. *About 4¹/₂ dozen cookies*

Puddings, Mousses & Soufflés

HOT CHOCOLATE SOUFFLÉ

³/₄ cup HERSHEY'S Cocoa
³/₄ cup sugar
¹/₂ cup unsifted all-purpose flour
¹/₄ teaspoon salt
2 cups milk
6 egg yolks, well beaten
2 tablespoons butter

1 teaspoon vanilla
8 egg whites, at room
  temperature
¹/₄ teaspoon cream of tartar
¹/₄ cup sugar
Sweetened whipped cream
  (optional)

Lightly butter 2¹/₂-quart soufflé dish; sprinkle with sugar. Measure length of heavy-duty aluminum foil to fit around soufflé dish; fold in thirds lengthwise. Lightly oil one side of collar; tape securely to outside of dish (oiled side in), allowing collar to extend at least 2 inches above rim. Set aside.

Combine cocoa, ³/₄ cup sugar, the flour and salt in medium saucepan; gradually blend in milk. Cook over medium heat, stirring constantly with wire whisk, until mixture boils; remove from heat. Gradually stir small amount of chocolate mixture into beaten egg yolks; blend well. Return egg mixture to chocolate mixture in pan. Add butter and vanilla, stirring until combined. Set aside; cool to lukewarm.

Beat egg whites with cream of tartar in large mixer bowl until soft peaks form. Add ¹/₄ cup sugar, 2 tablespoons at a time, beating until stiff peaks form. Gently fold one-third of the chocolate mixture into beaten egg whites. Fold in remaining chocolate mixture, half at a time, just until combined.

Gently pour mixture, without stirring, into prepared dish; smooth top with spatula. Place dish in larger pan; place in oven on bottom rack. Pour hot water

(continued)

Hot Chocolate Soufflé

into pan to depth of 1 inch (be sure bottom of foil collar does not touch water bath). Bake at 350° for 1 hour and 10 minutes or until cake tester inserted halfway between edge and center comes out clean. Carefully remove foil. Serve immediately with sweetened whipped cream. *8 to 10 servings*

Soufflé Success Tips

• To help the soufflé collar stand straight, fasten seam with tape. And be sure the bottom of the collar doesn't touch the water bath.

• Don't "overfold"! For a high, light soufflé, fold chocolate mixture into egg whites *very* gently.

STRAWBERRY-CHOCOLATE BAVARIAN CREAM

1 package (10 ounces) frozen
    sliced strawberries, thawed
2 envelopes unflavored gelatine
1/2 cup sugar
1 cup HERSHEY'S Semi-Sweet
    Chocolate Chips

2 1/4 cups milk
1 teaspoon vanilla
2 cups heavy or whipping cream
1 teaspoon vanilla
2 or 3 drops red food color

Drain strawberries; reserve syrup. Add water to syrup to equal 3/4 cup. Stir gelatine into liquid; set aside. Puree or mash berries to equal 1/2 cup; reserve.

Combine sugar, chocolate chips and 1/2 cup of the milk in medium saucepan. Cook over low heat, stirring constantly, until mixture is smooth and very hot. Add gelatine mixture, stirring until gelatine is dissolved. Remove from heat; add remaining 1 3/4 cups milk and 1 teaspoon vanilla. Pour into bowl; chill, stirring occasionally, until mixture mounds when dropped from a spoon.

Whip 1 cup of the cream until stiff; fold into chocolate mixture. Pour into oiled 5- or 6-cup mold; chill until firm. Whip remaining 1 cup cream and 1 teaspoon vanilla in small mixer bowl until stiff. Fold in reserved puree and food color. Unmold Bavarian; garnish with strawberry mixture. *8 to 10 servings*

DOUBLE CHOCOLATE MOUSSE

2 HERSHEY'S Milk Chocolate
    Bars (8 ounces each)
2 blocks (2 ounces) HERSHEY'S
    Unsweetened Baking
    Chocolate
5 tablespoons water
2 tablespoons rum or brandy

2 egg yolks
1/4 cup butter or margarine
1 cup heavy or whipping cream
18 ladyfingers, split
4 egg whites
    Chopped almonds (optional)

Break chocolate bars and baking chocolate into pieces. Melt with water and rum in top of double boiler over hot, not boiling, water; stir until mixture is smooth. Remove from heat; blend in egg yolks. Add butter, 1 tablespoon at a time, stirring until blended; cool slightly. Whip cream until stiff; carefully fold into chocolate mixture. Chill 1 hour or until mixture begins to set.

Meanwhile, line bottom and side of 8- or 9-inch springform pan with ladyfingers, rounded sides against pan. Beat egg whites until stiff but not dry. Carefully fold into chocolate mixture. Pour into ladyfinger-lined pan and chill 8 hours or overnight. Just before serving, remove side of pan. Sprinkle with chopped almonds; garnish as desired. *10 to 12 servings*

Top: Strawberry-Chocolate Bavarian Cream
Bottom: Double Chocolate Mousse

CHOCOLATE CREAM PUDDING

1 cup sugar
$^1/_4$ cup HERSHEY'S Cocoa
$^1/_3$ cup cornstarch
$^1/_4$ teaspoon salt
3 cups milk

3 egg yolks, slightly beaten
2 tablespoons butter or
  margarine
$1^1/_2$ teaspoons vanilla

Combine sugar, cocoa, cornstarch and salt in heavy saucepan; add milk and egg yolks. Cook over medium heat, stirring constantly, until mixture boils; boil and stir 1 minute. Remove from heat; blend in butter and vanilla. Pour into bowl or individual dessert dishes; press plastic wrap directly onto surface. Cool; chill until set.   *6 to 8 servings*

INDIVIDUAL FUDGE SOUFFLÉS

$^1/_2$ cup butter or margarine,
  softened
$1^1/_4$ cups sugar
1 teaspoon vanilla
4 eggs
$^2/_3$ cup milk
$^1/_2$ teaspoon instant coffee
  granules

$^2/_3$ cup unsifted all-purpose flour
$^2/_3$ cup HERSHEY'S Cocoa
$1^1/_2$ teaspoons baking powder
1 cup heavy or whipping cream
2 tablespoons confectioners'
  sugar

Grease and sugar eight 5- or 6-ounce custard cups or ramekins; set aside. Cream butter, sugar and vanilla in large mixer bowl until light and fluffy. Add eggs, one at a time, beating well after each addition. Scald milk; remove from heat and add coffee granules, stirring until dissolved. Combine flour, cocoa and baking powder; add alternately with milk-coffee mixture to creamed mixture. Beat 1 minute on medium speed.

Divide batter evenly among prepared custard cups. Place in two 8-inch square pans; place pans in oven. Pour hot water into pans to depth of $^1/_8$ inch. Bake at 325° for 40 to 45 minutes for custard cups (50 to 55 minutes for ramekins), adding more water if necessary, until cake tester inserted halfway between edge and center comes out clean. Remove pans from oven and allow custard cups to stand in water 5 minutes. Remove custard cups from water; cool slightly. Serve in custard cups or invert onto dessert dishes. Beat cream with confectioners' sugar until stiff; spoon onto warm soufflés.   *8 servings*

Chocolate Mousse à l'Orange

CHOCOLATE MOUSSE A L'ORANGE

2 cups (12-ounce package)
    HERSHEY'S Semi-Sweet
    Chocolate Chips
1 block (1 ounce) HERSHEY'S
    Unsweetened Baking
    Chocolate
6 tablespoons water
6 egg yolks, at room temperature

2 to 3 tablespoons orange-
    flavored liqueur
1¹/₂ cups heavy or whipping cream
6 egg whites, at room
    temperature
¹/₂ cup sugar
    Sweetened whipped cream
    Orange slices, cut into wedges
    (optional)

Melt chocolate chips and baking chocolate with water in top of double boiler over hot, not boiling, water; stir until smooth. Remove from heat. With wire whisk, beat egg yolks, one at a time, into chocolate mixture; cool to lukewarm. Stir in orange-flavored liqueur. Whip cream until stiff; fold into chocolate mixture.

Beat egg whites in large mixer bowl until foamy. Gradually add sugar; beat until stiff peaks form. Fold in chocolate-cream mixture. Spoon into dessert dishes. Cover; chill several hours or until firm. Garnish with sweetened whipped cream and orange wedges.   *16 servings*

Cold Mocha Soufflé

COLD MOCHA SOUFFLÉ

2 envelopes unflavored gelatine	1 cup heavy or whipping cream
¹/₂ cup sugar	3 egg whites, at room
¹/₃ cup HERSHEY'S Cocoa	temperature
1 tablespoon instant coffee	¹/₄ cup sugar
granules	Cozumel Whipped Cream
2¹/₄ cups milk	(optional)
3 egg yolks, beaten	Chocolate curls (optional)
¹/₂ teaspoon vanilla	

Measure length of aluminum foil to fit around 1-quart soufflé dish; fold in thirds lengthwise. Lightly oil one side of collar; tape securely to outside of dish (oiled side in), allowing collar to extend 3 inches above rim of dish. Set aside.

Combine gelatine, ¹/₂ cup sugar, the cocoa and coffee granules in medium saucepan; blend in milk and egg yolks. Let stand 2 minutes. Stir over low heat until gelatine is completely dissolved and mixture coats a metal spoon; *do not boil*. Remove from heat; add vanilla. Pour into large bowl and chill, stirring occasionally, until mixture mounds slightly when dropped from a spoon.

Whip cream until stiff; fold into chocolate mixture. Beat egg whites in small mixer bowl until soft peaks form; gradually add ¹/₄ cup sugar and beat until stiff peaks form. Fold into chocolate mixture. Pour into prepared dish; chill until set, at least 4 hours. Just before serving, carefully remove foil. Garnish with Cozumel Whipped Cream and chocolate curls.   *6 to 8 servings*
(continued)

COZUMEL WHIPPED CREAM

½ cup heavy or whipping cream
1 tablespoon confectioners' sugar

1 to 2 teaspoons coffee-flavored
    liqueur

Beat cream with confectioners' sugar in small bowl until stiff. Fold in coffee-flavored liqueur.

POTS DE CRÈME AU CHOCOLAT

2 blocks (2 ounces) HERSHEY'S
    Unsweetened Baking
    Chocolate, broken into pieces
1 cup light cream
⅔ cup sugar
2 egg yolks, slightly beaten

2 tablespoons butter or
    margarine, softened
1 teaspoon vanilla
    Sweetened whipped cream
    Candied violets (optional)

Combine baking chocolate pieces and cream in medium saucepan. Cook over medium heat, stirring constantly with wire whisk, until chocolate flecks disappear and mixture is hot. Add sugar and continue cooking and stirring until mixture begins to boil. Remove from heat; gradually add to beaten egg yolks, stirring constantly. Stir in butter and vanilla. Pour into six crème pots or demitasse cups; press plastic wrap directly onto surface. Chill several hours or until set. Garnish with sweetened whipped cream and candied violets.

6 servings

Pots de Crème au Chocolat

CHOCOLATE-BERRY PARFAITS

Chocolate Cream Pudding
(page 60)
1 package (10 ounces) frozen
sliced strawberries, thawed,
or 1 cup sweetened sliced
fresh strawberries

1 cup heavy or whipping cream*
1/4 cup confectioners' sugar*
Fresh strawberries (optional)

Prepare Chocolate Cream Pudding; cool completely. Drain strawberries; puree in blender or sieve to equal 1/2 to 3/4 cup. Beat cream and confectioners' sugar until stiff; fold in strawberry puree. Alternately layer chocolate pudding and strawberry cream in parfait glasses. Chill until set. Garnish with strawberries. *8 to 10 servings*

*You may substitute 2 cups frozen non-dairy whipped topping, thawed, for the cream and confectioners' sugar.

Chocolate-Berry Parfaits

MOCHA FUDGE PUDDING CAKE

3/4 cup sugar
1 cup unsifted all-purpose flour
2 teaspoons baking powder
1/4 teaspoon salt
1/2 cup butter or margarine
1 block (1 ounce) HERSHEY'S
    Unsweetened Baking
    Chocolate

1/2 cup milk
1 teaspoon vanilla
1/2 cup sugar
1/2 cup packed light brown sugar
1/4 cup HERSHEY'S Cocoa
1 cup hot strong coffee
Ice cream

Combine 3/4 cup sugar, the flour, baking powder and salt in medium bowl. Melt butter with baking chocolate in small saucepan over low heat; add to dry ingredients with milk and vanilla. Beat until smooth. Pour into 8- or 9-inch square pan.

Combine 1/2 cup sugar, the brown sugar and cocoa in small bowl; sprinkle evenly over batter. Pour coffee over top; *do not stir*. Bake at 350° for 40 minutes or until center is almost set. Serve warm with ice cream.

8 to 10 servings

COCOA BAVARIAN CREAM

2 envelopes unflavored gelatine
1 1/2 cups cold milk
1 1/4 cups sugar
3/4 cup HERSHEY'S Cocoa
1 tablespoon light corn syrup
3 tablespoons butter or
    margarine

1 3/4 cups milk
1 1/2 teaspoons vanilla
10 to 12 ladyfingers, split
1 cup heavy or whipping cream

Sprinkle gelatine onto 1 1/2 cups milk in medium saucepan; let stand 3 to 4 minutes to soften. Combine sugar and cocoa; add to gelatine mixture in saucepan. Add corn syrup. Cook over medium heat, stirring constantly, until mixture boils. Remove from heat; stir in butter until melted. Blend in 1 3/4 cups milk and the vanilla; pour into large mixer bowl. Cool; chill until almost set.

Meanwhile, line bottom and side of 1 1/2-quart mold with ladyfingers, rounded sides against mold. Whip cream until stiff. Beat chilled chocolate mixture until smooth. Add whipped cream to chocolate on low speed just until blended. Pour into ladyfinger-lined mold; chill until set. Unmold before serving.

12 servings

Candies

RICH COCOA FUDGE

3 cups sugar	1¹/₂ cups milk
²/₃ cup HERSHEY'S Cocoa	¹/₄ cup butter or margarine
¹/₈ teaspoon salt	1 teaspoon vanilla

Butter 8- or 9-inch square pan; set aside. Combine sugar, cocoa and salt in heavy 4-quart saucepan; stir in milk. Cook over medium heat, stirring constantly, until mixture comes to full rolling boil. Boil, without stirring, to soft-ball stage, 234°F on a candy thermometer (or until syrup, when dropped into very cold water, forms a soft ball that flattens when removed from water). Bulb of candy thermometer should not rest on bottom of saucepan.

Remove from heat. Add butter and vanilla; *do not stir*. Cool at room temperature to 110°F (lukewarm). Beat until fudge thickens and loses some of its gloss. Quickly spread in prepared pan; cool. Cut into 1- to 1¹/₂-inch squares.

About 3 dozen candies

VARIATIONS

Marshmallow-Nut Cocoa Fudge: Increase cocoa to ³/₄ cup. Cook fudge as directed. Add 1 cup marshmallow creme with butter and vanilla; *do not stir*. Cool to 110°F (lukewarm). Beat 10 minutes; stir in 1 cup broken nuts and pour into prepared pan. (Fudge does not set until poured into pan).

Nutty Rich Cocoa Fudge: Beat cooked fudge as directed. *Immediately* stir in 1 cup broken almonds, pecans or walnuts and quickly spread in prepared pan.

Center: Chocolate-Almond Fudge (see page 68)
Upper right: Double-Decker Fudge (see page 68)
Below: Nutty Rich Cocoa Fudge

DOUBLE-DECKER FUDGE

1 cup REESE'S Peanut Butter
　Chips
1 cup HERSHEY'S Semi-Sweet
　Chocolate Chips
2¹/₄ cups sugar

1³/₄ cups (7-ounce jar) marshmallow
　creme
³/₄ cup evaporated milk
¹/₄ cup butter or margarine
1 teaspoon vanilla

Measure peanut butter chips into one bowl and chocolate chips into another; set aside. Butter 8-inch square pan; set aside. Combine sugar, marshmallow creme, evaporated milk and butter in heavy 3-quart saucepan. Cook over medium heat, stirring constantly, until mixture boils; continue cooking and stirring for 5 minutes.

Remove from heat; stir in vanilla. Immediately stir half the hot mixture into peanut butter chips until completely melted. Quickly pour into prepared pan. Stir remaining hot mixture into chocolate chips until completely melted. Quickly spread over top of peanut butter layer; cool. Cut into 1-inch squares.

About 4 dozen candies

CHOCOLATE-ALMOND FUDGE

4 cups sugar
1³/₄ cups (7-ounce jar) marshmallow
　creme
1¹/₂ cups (12-ounce can) evaporated
　milk
1 tablespoon butter or margarine
2 cups (12-ounce package)
　HERSHEY'S MINI CHIPS
　Semi-Sweet Chocolate

1 HERSHEY'S Milk Chocolate
　Bar with Almonds
　(8 ounces), chopped
1 teaspoon vanilla
³/₄ cup chopped slivered almonds

Butter 9-inch square pan; set aside. Combine sugar, marshmallow creme, evaporated milk and butter in heavy 4-quart saucepan. Cook over medium heat, stirring constantly, until mixture comes to a full rolling boil; boil and stir 7 minutes. Remove from heat; *immediately* add MINI CHIPS Chocolates and chocolate bar pieces, stirring until completely melted. Blend in vanilla; stir in almonds. Pour into prepared pan; cool completely. Cut into 1-inch squares.

About 5 dozen candies

CHOCOLATE TRUFFLES

1/2 cup unsalted butter, softened
2 1/2 cups confectioners' sugar
1/2 cup HERSHEY'S Cocoa
1/4 cup heavy or whipping cream
1 1/2 teaspoons vanilla

Centers: Pecan or walnut
 halves, whole almonds,
 candied cherries, after-dinner
 mints
Coatings: Confectioners' sugar,
 flaked coconut, chopped nuts

Cream butter in large mixer bowl. Combine 2 1/2 cups confectioners' sugar and the cocoa; add alternately with cream and vanilla to butter. Blend well. Chill until firm. Shape small amount of mixture around desired center; roll into 1-inch balls. Drop into desired coating and turn until well covered. Chill until firm. *About 3 dozen truffles*

VARIATION
Chocolate Rum Truffles: Decrease vanilla to 1 teaspoon and add 1/2 teaspoon rum extract.

COCOA DIVINITY

3 tablespoons shortening
1/2 cup HERSHEY'S Cocoa
2 1/2 cups sugar
1/4 teaspoon salt
1/2 cup light corn syrup

1/3 cup water
2 egg whites, at room
 temperature
1 teaspoon vanilla
3/4 cup chopped walnuts (optional)

Melt shortening in top of double boiler over hot, not boiling, water; add cocoa and stir until smooth. Set aside over warm water. Combine sugar, salt, corn syrup and water in heavy 2-quart saucepan. Cook over medium heat, stirring constantly, until sugar dissolves and mixture boils. Continue to boil without stirring. When syrup reaches 246°F on a candy thermometer, start beating egg whites in large mixer bowl until stiff peaks form. (Bulb of candy thermometer should not rest on bottom of saucepan.)

Continue cooking syrup mixture, without stirring, to hard-ball stage, 260°F (or until syrup, when dropped into very cold water, forms a firm ball that is hard enough to hold its shape, yet plastic). Immediately pour hot syrup in thin stream over beaten egg whites, beating constantly on high speed. Add vanilla; beat until candy starts to become firm. Quickly blend in reserved cocoa mixture with wooden spoon. Stir in nuts. Drop by teaspoonfuls onto wax paper-covered cookie sheet; cool. Store in airtight container. *About 3 1/2 dozen candies*

CHOCOLATE CHIP NOUGAT LOG

1 cup sugar
2/3 cup light corn syrup
2 tablespoons water
1/4 cup egg whites (about 2), at
  room temperature
2 cups sugar
1 1/4 cups light corn syrup

1/4 cup butter or margarine,
  melted
2 teaspoons vanilla
2 cups chopped walnuts
4 or 5 drops red food color
  (optional)
1 cup HERSHEY'S MINI CHIPS
  Semi-Sweet Chocolate

Line 15 1/2 × 10 1/2 × 1-inch jelly roll pan with aluminum foil; butter foil. Set aside. Combine 1 cup sugar, 2/3 cup corn syrup and the water in small heavy saucepan. Cook over medium heat, stirring constantly, until sugar dissolves. Continue cooking without stirring. When syrup reaches 230°F on a candy thermometer, start beating egg whites in large mixer bowl; beat until stiff, but not dry. (Bulb of candy thermometer should not rest on bottom of saucepan.)

When syrup reaches soft-ball stage, 238°F (or until syrup, when dropped into very cold water, forms a soft ball that flattens when removed from water), remove from heat. Pour hot syrup in thin stream over beaten egg whites, beating constantly on high speed. Continue beating 4 to 5 minutes or until mixture becomes very thick. Cover and set aside.

Combine 2 cups sugar and 1 1/4 cups corn syrup in heavy 2-quart saucepan. Cook over medium heat, stirring constantly, until sugar dissolves. Cook, without stirring, to soft-crack stage, 275°F (or until syrup, when dropped into very cold water, separates into threads that are hard but not brittle).

Pour hot syrup all at once over reserved egg white mixture in bowl; blend with wooden spoon. Stir in melted butter and vanilla; add nuts and mix thoroughly. Add food color. Pour into prepared pan. Sprinkle evenly with MINI CHIPS Chocolates. Let cool overnight.

To form logs, invert pan and remove foil. Cut in half crosswise; roll from cut end, jelly-roll style. Cut into 1/4-inch slices. Store, well covered, in cool, dry place. *About 7 dozen candies*

Note: If desired, nougat can be cut into 1-inch squares rather than rolled.

Top: Chocolate Chip Nougat Log. Bottom: Butter Almond Crunch (see page 72).
Center: Assortment includes Cocoa Divinity (see page 69) and Creamy Cocoa Taffy (see page 72).

BUTTER ALMOND CRUNCH

1½ cups HERSHEY'S MINI CHIPS
    Semi-Sweet Chocolate
1¾ cups chopped almonds
1½ cups butter or margarine

1¾ cups sugar
3 tablespoons light corn syrup
3 tablespoons water

Spread 1 cup of the MINI CHIPS Chocolates in buttered 13 × 9-inch pan; set aside. Spread almonds in shallow pan; toast at 350° for about 7 minutes or until golden brown. Set aside.

Melt butter in heavy 3-quart saucepan; blend in sugar, corn syrup and water. Cook over medium heat, stirring constantly, to hard-crack stage, 300°F on a candy thermometer (or until syrup, when dropped into very cold water, separates into threads that are hard and brittle). Bulb of candy thermometer should not rest on bottom of saucepan. Remove saucepan from heat; stir in 1½ cups of the toasted almonds.

Immediately spread mixture evenly over MINI CHIPS Chocolates in prepared pan, being careful not to disturb chips. Sprinkle with remaining ¼ cup toasted almonds and ½ cup MINI CHIPS Chocolates; score into 1½-inch squares. Cool completely; remove from pan. Break into pieces. Store in tightly covered container. *About 2 pounds candy*

CREAMY COCOA TAFFY

1¼ cups sugar
¾ cup light corn syrup
⅓ cup HERSHEY'S Cocoa
⅛ teaspoon salt

2 teaspoons white vinegar
¼ cup evaporated milk
1 tablespoon butter or margarine

Butter 9-inch square pan; set aside. Combine sugar, corn syrup, cocoa, salt and vinegar in heavy 2-quart saucepan. Cook over medium heat, stirring constantly, until mixture boils; add evaporated milk and butter. Continue to cook, stirring occasionally, to firm-ball stage, 248°F on a candy thermometer (or until syrup, when dropped into very cold water, forms a firm ball that does not flatten when removed from water). Bulb of candy thermometer should not rest on bottom of saucepan.

Pour mixture into prepared pan. Let stand until taffy is cool enough to handle. Butter hands; stretch taffy, folding and pulling until light in color and hard to pull. Place taffy on table; pull into ½-inch-wide strips (twist two strips together, if desired). Cut into 1-inch pieces with buttered scissors. Wrap individually in plastic wrap. *About 1¼ pounds candy*

Breads & Coffeecakes

CHOCOLATE CHIP PANCAKES

2 cups buttermilk baking mix
1 cup milk
2 eggs

$^{1}/_{2}$ cup HERSHEY'S MINI CHIPS
Semi-Sweet Chocolate

Combine buttermilk baking mix, milk and eggs in medium bowl; beat with wooden spoon until smooth. Stir in MINI CHIPS Chocolates. For each pancake, pour 2 tablespoons batter onto hot, lightly greased griddle; cook until bubbles appear. Turn; cook other side until lightly browned. (For thinner pancakes, add 1 tablespoon milk to batter; pancakes should be at least $^{1}/_{4}$ inch thick.) Serve warm with butter or margarine; sprinkle with confectioners' sugar or top with syrup.   *About 18 pancakes*

CHOCOLATE WAFFLES

1 cup unsifted all-purpose flour
$^{3}/_{4}$ cup sugar
$^{1}/_{2}$ cup HERSHEY'S Cocoa
$^{1}/_{2}$ teaspoon baking powder
$^{1}/_{2}$ teaspoon baking soda

$^{1}/_{4}$ teaspoon salt
1 cup buttermilk
2 eggs
$^{1}/_{4}$ cup butter or margarine,
melted

Combine flour, sugar, cocoa, baking powder, baking soda and salt in medium bowl. Add buttermilk and eggs; beat with wooden spoon just until blended. Gradually add melted butter, beating until smooth. Bake in waffle iron according to manufacturer's directions. Serve warm with pancake syrup or, for dessert, with ice cream, fruit-flavored syrups and sweetened whipped cream.
10 to 12 four-inch waffles

COCOA BRUNCH RINGS

¹/₂ cup milk	2 eggs, slightly beaten
¹/₂ cup sugar	3¹/₂ to 3³/₄ cups unsifted
1 teaspoon salt	all-purpose flour
¹/₂ cup butter or margarine	³/₄ cup HERSHEY'S Cocoa
2 packages active dry yeast	Orange Filling
¹/₂ cup warm water	

Scald milk in small saucepan; stir in sugar, salt and butter. Set aside; cool to lukewarm. Dissolve yeast in warm water (105° to 115°F) in large mixer bowl; add milk mixture, eggs and 2 cups of the flour. Beat 2 minutes on medium speed until smooth. Combine 1¹/₂ cups of the flour and the cocoa; stir into yeast mixture.

Turn dough out onto well-floured board; knead in more flour until dough is smooth enough to handle. Knead about 5 minutes or until smooth and elastic. Place in greased bowl; turn to grease top. Cover; let rise in warm place until doubled, about 1 to 1¹/₂ hours. Punch down dough; turn over. Cover; let rise 30 minutes longer.

Prepare Orange Filling; set aside. Divide dough in half. On lightly floured board, roll out each half to a 13×9-inch rectangle. Spread one-fourth of the Orange Filling on each rectangle to within ¹/₂ inch of edges; reserve remaining filling for frosting. Roll up dough from long side as for jelly roll; pinch edge to seal. Cut rolls into 1-inch slices. Place slices, sealed edges down, in two greased 4- to 6-cup ring molds. Tilt slices slightly, overlapping so filling shows. Cover; let rise in warm place until doubled, about 45 minutes. Bake at 350° for 20 to 25 minutes or until filling is lightly browned. Immediately remove from molds and place on serving plates. Frost with remaining Orange Filling or, if a glaze is preferred, stir in a few drops orange juice until of desired consistency; spoon over rings. Serve warm.   *2 rings*

ORANGE FILLING

3 cups confectioners' sugar	¹/₄ cup orange juice
6 tablespoons butter or	4 teaspoons grated orange peel
margarine, softened	

Combine confectioners' sugar, butter, orange juice and orange peel in small mixer bowl; beat on low speed until smooth.

Top: Cocoa Brunch Ring
Bottom: Chocolate-Filled Braid (see page 76)

CHOCOLATE-FILLED BRAID

Chocolate Filling
2¹/₂ to 2³/₄ cups unsifted
  all-purpose flour
2 tablespoons sugar
¹/₂ teaspoon salt
1 package active dry yeast
¹/₂ cup milk

¹/₄ cup water
¹/₂ cup butter or margarine
1 egg, at room temperature
Melted butter (optional)
Confectioners' Sugar Glaze
  (optional)

Prepare Chocolate Filling; set aside. Combine 1 cup of the flour, the sugar, salt and yeast in large mixer bowl; set aside. Combine milk, water and ¹/₂ cup butter in small saucepan; cook over low heat until liquids are very warm (120° to 130°F)—butter does not need to melt. Gradually add to dry ingredients; beat 2 minutes on medium speed. Add egg and ¹/₂ cup of the flour; beat 2 minutes on high speed. Stir in enough additional flour to make a stiff dough. Cover; allow to rest 20 minutes.

Turn dough out onto well-floured board; roll into 18×10-inch rectangle. Spread Chocolate Filling lengthwise down center third of dough. Cut 1-inch-wide strips diagonally along both sides of filling to within ³/₄ inch of filling. Alternately fold opposite strips of dough at an angle across filling. Carefully transfer to greased cookie sheet. Shape into ring, stretching slightly; pinch ends together. Cover loosely with wax paper brushed with vegetable oil; top with plastic wrap. Chill at least 2 hours or overnight.

Let dough stand, uncovered, at room temperature 10 minutes. Bake at 375° for 30 to 35 minutes or until lightly browned. Remove from cookie sheet; cool completely on wire rack. Brush with melted butter or drizzle with Confectioners' Sugar Glaze. *10 to 12 servings*

CHOCOLATE FILLING

³/₄ cup HERSHEY'S Semi-Sweet
  Chocolate Chips
2 tablespoons sugar
¹/₃ cup evaporated milk

¹/₂ cup finely chopped nuts
1 teaspoon vanilla
¹/₄ teaspoon cinnamon

Combine chocolate chips, sugar and evaporated milk in small saucepan. Cook over low heat, stirring constantly, until chips melt and mixture is smooth. Stir in nuts, vanilla and cinnamon. Cool.

CONFECTIONERS' SUGAR GLAZE

1 cup confectioners' sugar
1 tablespoon butter or margarine,
  softened

¹/₂ teaspoon vanilla
1 to 2 tablespoons milk

Beat confectioners' sugar, butter, vanilla and milk in small mixer bowl until glaze is smooth and of desired consistency.

MOCHA-CHIP COFFEECAKE

Streusel Topping
2 cups buttermilk baking mix
2 tablespoons sugar
1 tablespoon instant coffee
   granules

²/₃ cup milk
1 egg
1 cup HERSHEY'S MINI CHIPS
   Semi-Sweet Chocolate

Prepare Streusel Topping; set aside. Combine baking mix, sugar, coffee granules, milk and egg in large bowl; beat vigorously with wooden spoon for 30 seconds. Spread half the batter in greased 8-inch round pan; sprinkle with half the MINI CHIPS Chocolates and half the Streusel Topping. Cover with remaining batter; repeat layers of MINI CHIPS Chocolates and topping. Bake at 400° for 25 to 30 minutes or until cake tester comes out clean. Serve warm.

About 6 servings

STREUSEL TOPPING

¹/₃ cup buttermilk baking mix
¹/₃ cup packed light brown sugar
¹/₂ teaspoon cinnamon

2 tablespoons butter or
   margarine, softened

Using fork or pastry blender, combine baking mix, brown sugar, cinnamon and butter in small bowl until crumbly.

Mocha-Chip Coffeecake

Clockwise from top: Chocolate Chip Muffins, Chocolate Tea Bread and Chocolate Chip Banana Bread

CHOCOLATE CHIP BANANA BREAD

2 cups unsifted all-purpose flour
1 cup sugar
1 teaspoon baking powder
1 teaspoon salt
1/2 teaspoon baking soda
1 cup mashed ripe bananas
   (about 3 small)

1/2 cup shortening
2 eggs
1 cup HERSHEY'S MINI CHIPS
   Semi-Sweet Chocolate
1/2 cup chopped walnuts

(continued)

Grease bottom only of 9×5×3-inch loaf pan; set aside. Combine all ingredients except MINI CHIPS Chocolates and walnuts in large mixer bowl; blend well on medium speed. Stir in MINI CHIPS Chocolates and walnuts.

Pour into prepared pan. Bake at 350° for 60 to 70 minutes or until cake tester comes out clean. Cool 10 minutes; remove from pan. Cool completely on wire rack.   *1 loaf*

CHOCOLATE CHIP MUFFINS

1¹/₂ cups unsifted all-purpose flour
¹/₂ cup sugar
  2 teaspoons baking powder
¹/₂ teaspoon salt
¹/₂ cup milk
¹/₄ cup vegetable oil
  1 egg, beaten

¹/₂ cup HERSHEY'S MINI CHIPS
    Semi-Sweet Chocolate
¹/₂ cup chopped nuts
¹/₄ cup chopped maraschino
    cherries, well drained
  2 teaspoons grated orange peel

Combine flour, sugar, baking powder and salt in medium bowl. Add milk, oil and egg; stir just until blended. Stir in MINI CHIPS Chocolates, nuts, cherries and orange peel.

Fill greased or paper-lined muffin cups (2¹/₂ inches in diameter) two-thirds full with batter. Bake at 400° for 25 to 30 minutes or until golden brown. Remove from pan; cool completely.   *About 12 muffins*

CHOCOLATE TEA BREAD

¹/₄ cup butter or margarine,
    softened
²/₃ cup sugar
  1 egg
1¹/₂ cups unsifted all-purpose flour
¹/₃ cup HERSHEY'S Cocoa

  1 teaspoon baking soda
¹/₄ teaspoon salt
  1 cup buttermilk or sour milk*
³/₄ cup chopped walnuts
³/₄ cup raisins (optional)

Cream butter, sugar and egg in large mixer bowl until light and fluffy. Combine flour, cocoa, baking soda and salt; add alternately with buttermilk to creamed mixture. Beat on low speed just until blended; stir in nuts and raisins.

Pour into greased 8¹/₂×4¹/₂×2¹/₂-inch loaf pan. Bake at 350° for 55 to 60 minutes or until cake tester comes out clean. Remove from pan; cool completely on wire rack.   *1 loaf*

*To sour milk: Use 1 tablespoon vinegar plus milk to equal 1 cup.

Microwave Specialties

MICROWAVE HERSHEY BAR PIE

Chocolate Crumb Crust or
Graham Cracker Crust (page
38)
1 HERSHEY'S Milk Chocolate
Bar (8 ounces), broken into
pieces

$^1/_3$ cup milk
$1^1/_2$ cups miniature marshmallows
1 cup heavy or whipping cream
Sweetened whipped cream
Chilled cherry pie filling

Bake crumb crust; set aside. Combine chocolate bar pieces, milk and miniature marshmallows in medium micro-proof bowl. Microwave at HIGH (100%) for $1^1/_2$ to $2^1/_2$ minutes or until chocolate is softened and mixture is melted and smooth when stirred. Cool completely.

Whip cream until stiff; fold into chocolate mixture. Spoon into crust. Cover; chill several hours or until firm. Garnish with sweetened whipped cream; serve with chilled cherry pie filling. *8 servings*

CHOCOLATE CRUMB CRUST

$^1/_2$ cup butter or margarine
$1^1/_2$ cups graham cracker crumbs

6 tablespoons HERSHEY'S Cocoa
$^1/_3$ cup confectioners' sugar

Grease micro-proof 9-inch pie plate. In small micro-proof bowl, microwave butter at HIGH (100%) for 1 minute or until melted. Stir in graham cracker crumbs, cocoa and confectioners' sugar until well blended. Press on bottom and up side of prepared pie plate. Microwave an additional 1 to $1^1/_2$ minutes until bubbly. (Do not overcook.) Cool completely before filling.

Top: Microwave Hershey Bar Pie
Bottom: Crème de Cacao Pie (see page 82)

CRÈME DE CACAO PIE

9-inch pastry shell
1 envelope unflavored gelatine
1/2 cup cold milk
1/4 cup butter or margarine
1/3 cup sugar

6 tablespoons HERSHEY'S Cocoa
3 egg yolks, slightly beaten
1/4 cup crème de cacao
3 egg whites
1/3 cup sugar

Bake pastry shell; set aside. Sprinkle gelatine onto cold milk in small bowl; let stand 5 minutes to soften. Microwave butter in micro-proof bowl at HIGH (100%) for 30 to 60 seconds or until melted; stir in 1/3 cup sugar and the cocoa. Add gelatine mixture; blend well. Stir in beaten egg yolks; blend well. Microwave at MEDIUM (50%) for 2 1/2 to 3 1/2 minutes, stirring frequently, or until mixture is hot; *do not boil*. Stir in crème de cacao; cool.

Beat egg whites in large mixer bowl until foamy; gradually add 1/3 cup sugar, beating until stiff peaks form. Fold into chocolate mixture; pour into cooled shell. Cover; chill until firm. Garnish as desired. *8 servings*

MICROWAVE HERSHEY BAR MOUSSE

1 HERSHEY'S Milk Chocolate
    Bar (8 ounces), broken into
    pieces)

1/4 cup water
2 eggs, beaten
1 cup heavy or whipping cream

Combine chocolate bar pieces and water in medium micro-proof bowl. Microwave at HIGH (100%) for 1 1/2 to 2 minutes or until chocolate is softened and mixture is melted and smooth when stirred. Stir in eggs. Microwave at MEDIUM (50%) for 1 1/2 to 2 1/2 minutes or until mixture is hot; *do not boil*. Cool slightly. Whip cream until stiff; fold into cooled chocolate mixture. Pour into 8-inch square pan. Cover; freeze until firm. Cut into squares. *4 servings*

A Note About Microwave Ovens

Because microwave ovens vary in wattage and power output, cooking times given for microwave recipes may need to be adjusted. It is best to rely on the desired result ("until mixture boils," for example) as well as the recommended cooking time to determine doneness. Results were found to be most consistent if food was stirred or rotated several times during microwave cooking, even if cooked in a turntable-type microwave oven. All recipes were tested in several different brands/models of microwave ovens.

Top: Chocolate Chip Bran Muffins. Bottom: Cocoa Applesauce Muffins (see page 84).

CHOCOLATE CHIP BRAN MUFFINS

1¹/₂ cups bran flakes cereal
¹/₂ cup boiling water
1 cup buttermilk or sour milk*
¹/₄ cup vegetable oil
1 egg, slightly beaten
1¹/₄ cups unsifted all-purpose flour
¹/₂ cup sugar

1 teaspoon baking soda
¹/₄ teaspoon salt
¹/₂ cup HERSHEY'S MINI CHIPS
Semi-Sweet Chocolate
¹/₄ cup finely chopped dried
apricots
³/₄ cup bran flakes cereal

Combine 1¹/₂ cups bran flakes cereal and boiling water in medium bowl; blend well. Cool. Add buttermilk, oil and egg; blend well. Combine flour, sugar, baking soda and salt in medium bowl; stir in cereal mixture, MINI CHIPS Chocolates and apricots just until dry ingredients are moistened.

Place 6 paper muffin cups (2¹/₂ inches in diameter) in microwave cupcake or muffin maker or in 6-ounce micro-proof custard cups. Fill each cup half full with batter. Sprinkle 2 teaspoons bran flakes cereal on top of each muffin. Microwave at HIGH (100%) for 2¹/₂ to 3¹/₂ minutes, turning ¹/₄ turn at end of each minute, or until cake tester comes out clean. (Tops may still appear moist.) Let stand several minutes. (Moist spots will disappear upon standing.) Repeat cooking procedure with remaining batter. Serve warm.

About 1¹/₂ dozen muffins

*To sour milk: Use 1 tablespoon vinegar plus milk to equal 1 cup.

COCOA APPLESAUCE MUFFINS

Crunch Topping
1/4 cup HERSHEY'S Cocoa
1/4 cup vegetable oil
3/4 cup applesauce
1 egg, beaten
1 1/4 cups unsifted all-purpose flour

3/4 cup sugar
3/4 teaspoon baking soda
1/4 teaspoon salt
1/4 teaspoon cinnamon
1/2 cup chopped nuts

Prepare Crunch Topping; set aside. Combine cocoa and oil in small bowl; stir until smooth. Add applesauce and egg; blend well. Combine flour, sugar, baking soda, salt and cinnamon in medium bowl; stir in applesauce mixture and nuts just until dry ingredients are moistened.

Place 6 paper muffin cups (2 1/2 inches in diameter) in microwave cupcake or muffin maker or in 6-ounce micro-proof custard cups. Fill each cup half full with batter. Sprinkle about 2 teaspoons Crunch Topping on top of each muffin. Microwave at HIGH (100%) for 2 1/2 to 3 1/2 minutes, turning 1/4 turn at end of each minute, or until cake tester comes out clean. (Tops may still appear moist.) Let stand several minutes. (Moist spots will disappear upon standing.) Repeat cooking procedure with remaining batter. Serve warm.

12 to 14 muffins

CRUNCH TOPPING

1 tablespoon butter or margarine
2 tablespoons HERSHEY'S Cocoa
1/4 cup packed light brown sugar

1/4 cup chopped nuts
2 tablespoons flour
1/4 teaspoon cinnamon

Microwave butter in small micro-proof bowl at HIGH (100%) for 15 seconds or until melted; add cocoa and blend until smooth. Stir in brown sugar, nuts, flour and cinnamon.

MICROWAVE HOT COCOA

5 tablespoons sugar
3 tablespoons HERSHEY'S Cocoa
Dash salt

3 tablespoons hot water
2 cups milk
1/4 teaspoon vanilla

Combine sugar, cocoa, salt and hot water in 1-quart micro-proof measuring cup. Microwave at HIGH (100%) for 1 to 1 1/2 minutes or until boiling. Add milk; stir and microwave an additional 1 1/2 to 2 minutes or until hot. Stir in vanilla; blend well.

4 servings

One serving: Place 2 heaping teaspoons sugar, 1 heaping teaspoon HERSHEY'S Cocoa and dash salt in micro-proof cup. Add 2 teaspoons cold milk; stir until smooth. Fill cup with milk; microwave at HIGH (100%) for 1 to 1 1/2 minutes or until hot. Stir to blend.

PEANUTTY CHOCOLATE SNACK SQUARES

5 graham crackers, broken into
  squares
1/2 cup sugar
1 cup light corn syrup

1 cup HERSHEY'S Semi-Sweet
  Chocolate Chips
1 cup peanut butter
1 cup dry roasted peanuts

Line bottom of 8-inch square pan with graham cracker squares, cutting to fit as necessary. Combine sugar and corn syrup in 2-quart micro-proof bowl. Microwave at HIGH (100%), stirring every 2 minutes, until mixture boils; boil 3 minutes. Stir in chocolate chips, peanut butter and peanuts. Pour over crackers; spread carefully. Cover; refrigerate until firm. Cut into 2-inch squares.

16 squares

MICROWAVE CLASSIC CHOCOLATE SAUCE

2 blocks (2 ounces) HERSHEY'S
  Unsweetened Baking
  Chocolate
2 tablespoons butter or
  margarine

1 cup sugar
1/4 teaspoon salt
3/4 cup evaporated milk
1/2 teaspoon vanilla

Place baking chocolate and butter in small micro-proof bowl. Microwave at HIGH (100%) for 1 minute or until chocolate is softened and mixture is melted and smooth when stirred. Add sugar, salt and evaporated milk; blend well. Microwave an additional 2 to 3 minutes, stirring with wire whisk after each minute, or until mixture is smooth and hot. Stir in vanilla. Serve warm.

About 1 1/2 cups sauce

EASIEST-EVER COCOA FUDGE

3 2/3 cups (1-pound package)
  confectioners' sugar, sifted
1/2 cup HERSHEY'S Cocoa
1/2 cup butter or margarine, cut
  into pieces

1/4 cup milk
1/2 cup chopped nuts (optional)
1 tablespoon vanilla

Combine confectioners' sugar, cocoa, butter and milk in medium micro-proof bowl. Microwave at HIGH (100%) for 2 to 3 minutes or until butter is melted. Stir until mixture is smooth. Stir in nuts and vanilla; blend well. Spread evenly in buttered 8-inch square pan; cool. Cut into 1-inch squares.

About 5 dozen candies

Clockwise from top: Easy Rocky Road, Fast Chocolate-Pecan Fudge and Chocolate Crackles

CHOCOLATE CRACKLES

10 tablespoons butter or
    margarine
6 tablespoons HERSHEY'S Cocoa
1 cup sugar
2 teaspoons baking powder
1/2 teaspoon salt

2 eggs
1 teaspoon vanilla
2 cups unsifted all-purpose flour
1/2 cup chopped nuts
    Confectioners' sugar

Microwave butter in medium micro-proof bowl at HIGH (100%) for 45 to 60 seconds or until melted. Add cocoa; blend well. Beat in sugar, baking powder, salt, eggs and vanilla. Stir in flour and nuts. Refrigerate at least 8 hours or until firm.

Shape dough into 1-inch balls; roll in confectioners' sugar. Cover micro-proof plate with wax paper. Place 8 balls 2 inches apart in circular shape on wax paper. Microwave at MEDIUM (50%) for 1 1/2 to 2 minutes or until surface is dry but cookies are soft when touched. Cool on wax paper on countertop. Repeat cooking procedure with remaining dough. Before serving, sprinkle with additional confectioners' sugar.   *About 4 dozen cookies*

EASY ROCKY ROAD

2 cups (12-ounce package)
   HERSHEY'S Semi-Sweet
   Chocolate Chips
1/4 cup butter or margarine

2 tablespoons shortening
6 cups (10 1/2-ounce bag)
   miniature marshmallows
1/2 cup chopped nuts

Place chocolate chips, butter and shortening in large micro-proof bowl. Microwave at MEDIUM (50%) for 5 to 7 minutes or until chips are softened and mixture is melted and smooth when stirred. Add marshmallows and nuts; blend well. Spread evenly in buttered 8-inch square pan. Cover; chill until firm. Cut into 2-inch squares.

16 squares

FAST CHOCOLATE-PECAN FUDGE

1/2 cup butter or margarine
3/4 cup HERSHEY'S Cocoa
4 cups confectioners' sugar
1 teaspoon vanilla

1/2 cup evaporated milk
1 cup pecan pieces
Pecan halves (optional)

Microwave butter in 2-quart micro-proof bowl at HIGH (100%) for 1 to 1 1/2 minutes or until melted. Add cocoa; stir until smooth. Stir in confectioners' sugar and vanilla; blend well (mixture will be dry and crumbly). Stir in evaporated milk. Microwave at HIGH (100%) for 1 minute; stir. Microwave an additional 30 to 60 seconds or until mixture is hot. Stir mixture until smooth; add pecan pieces.

Pour into aluminum-foil-lined 8- or 9-inch square pan. Garnish with pecan halves. Cover; chill until firm, about 2 hours. Cut into 1-inch squares. Store, covered, in refrigerator.

About 4 dozen candies

EASY HOT FUDGE SAUCE

1/2 cup HERSHEY'S Cocoa
1 1/3 cups (14-ounce can) sweetened
   condensed milk*

3 tablespoons milk
1 tablespoon butter or margarine
1 teaspoon vanilla

Combine cocoa, sweetened condensed milk and milk in medium micro-proof bowl. Microwave at HIGH (100%) for 1 minute; stir. Microwave an additional 1 to 1 1/2 minutes, stirring occasionally with wire whisk, until mixture is smooth and hot. Stir in butter and vanilla. Serve warm.

About 1 1/2 cups sauce

*Do not use evaporated milk.

Sauces & Frostings

CHOCOLATE-COCONUT FROSTING

⅓ cup sugar
1 tablespoon cornstarch
¾ cup evaporated milk
1 HERSHEY'S Milk Chocolate
    Bar (4 ounces), broken into
    pieces

1 tablespoon butter or margarine
1 cup flaked coconut
½ cup chopped nuts

Combine sugar and cornstarch in small saucepan; blend in evaporated milk. Cook over medium heat, stirring constantly, until mixture boils; remove from heat. Add chocolate bar pieces and butter; stir until chocolate is melted and mixture is smooth. Stir in coconut and nuts. Immediately spread on cake.

About 2 cups frosting

ROYAL GLAZE

8 blocks (8 ounces) HERSHEY'S
    Semi-Sweet Baking
    Chocolate, broken into
    pieces*

½ cup heavy or whipping cream

Combine chocolate and cream in small saucepan. Cook over very low heat, stirring constantly, until chocolate is melted and mixture is smooth; *do not boil*. Remove from heat; cool, stirring occasionally, until mixture begins to thicken, about 10 to 15 minutes.

About 1 cup

*You may substitute 1⅓ cups HERSHEY'S Semi-Sweet Chocolate Chips for the baking chocolate.

Mt. Gretna Chocolate Fondue

MT. GRETNA CHOCOLATE FONDUE

4 blocks (4 ounces) HERSHEY'S
   Unsweetened Baking
   Chocolate
1 cup light cream

1 cup sugar
1/4 cup creamy peanut butter
1 1/2 teaspoons vanilla
Fondue Dippers

Combine chocolate and cream in medium saucepan. Cook over low heat, stirring constantly, until chocolate is melted and mixture is smooth. Add sugar and peanut butter; continue cooking until slightly thickened. Remove from heat; stir in vanilla. Pour into fondue pot or chafing dish; serve warm with Fondue Dippers. *About 2 cups fondue*

FONDUE DIPPERS
In advance, prepare a selection of the following: marshmallows; angel food, sponge or pound cake pieces; strawberries; grapes; pineapple chunks; mandarin orange segments; cherries; fresh fruit slices. (Drain fruit well. Brush fresh fruit with lemon juice to prevent fruit from turning brown.)

CHOCOLATE NUT SAUCE

1/3 cup butter or margarine
2/3 cup coarsely chopped pecans or
  almonds
1 1/3 cups sugar

1/2 cup HERSHEY'S Cocoa
1/4 teaspoon salt
1 cup light cream
3/4 teaspoon vanilla

Melt butter in medium saucepan over low heat; sauté chopped nuts in melted butter until lightly browned. Remove from heat; stir in sugar, cocoa and salt. Add cream; blend well. Cook over low heat, stirring constantly, until mixture just begins to boil. Remove from heat; add vanilla. Serve warm.

About 2 cups sauce

CHOCOLATE-PEPPERMINT TOPPING

1 cup frozen non-dairy whipped
  topping, thawed

3 tablespoons HERSHEY'S Syrup
4 drops peppermint extract

Combine whipped topping, syrup and peppermint extract in small bowl; blend well. A particularly good topping for angel food cake.

About 1 cup topping

HOT FUDGE SAUCE

3/4 cup sugar
1/2 cup HERSHEY'S Cocoa
2/3 cup evaporated milk

1/3 cup light corn syrup
1/3 cup butter or margarine
1 teaspoon vanilla

Combine sugar and cocoa in medium saucepan; blend in evaporated milk and corn syrup. Cook over low heat, stirring constantly, until mixture boils; boil and stir 1 minute. Remove from heat; stir in butter and vanilla. Serve warm.

About 2 cups sauce

Note: This sauce can be refrigerated for later use. Reheat in saucepan over very low heat, stirring constantly.

Top right: Chocolate Nut Sauce
Center left: Chocolate-Peppermint Topping
Bottom: Hot Fudge Sauce

CHOCOLATE BUTTERCREAM FROSTING

	1 cup frosting	2 cups frosting
Confectioners' sugar	1 cup	2²/₃ cups
HERSHEY'S Cocoa		
For light flavor	2 tablespoons	¹/₄ cup
For medium flavor	¹/₄ cup	¹/₂ cup
For dark flavor	¹/₃ cup	³/₄ cup
Butter or margarine, softened	3 tablespoons	6 tablespoons
Milk	2 tablespoons	4 to 5 tablespoons
Vanilla	¹/₂ teaspoon	1 teaspoon

In small bowl, combine confectioners' sugar with amount of cocoa for flavor you prefer. Cream butter and ¹/₂ cup cocoa mixture in small mixer bowl. Add remaining cocoa mixture, milk and vanilla; beat to spreading consistency. For a glossier texture, add 1 tablespoon light corn syrup to the mixture.

CHOCOLATE FUDGE FROSTING

	1 cup frosting	2 cups frosting
Butter or margarine	3 tablespoons	¹/₃ cup
HERSHEY'S Cocoa		
For light flavor	2 tablespoons	3 tablespoons
For medium flavor	¹/₄ cup	¹/₃ cup
For dark flavor	¹/₂ cup	²/₃ cup
Confectioners' sugar	1¹/₃ cups	2²/₃ cups
Milk	2 to 3 tablespoons	¹/₃ cup
Vanilla	¹/₂ teaspoon	1 teaspoon

Melt butter in small saucepan over medium heat. Add amount of cocoa for flavor you prefer. Cook over medium heat, stirring constantly, until mixture just begins to boil. Remove from heat. Pour into small mixer bowl; cool completely. Add confectioners' sugar alternately with milk, beating to spreading consistency. Blend in vanilla.

QUICK CHOCOLATE FROSTING

4 blocks (4 ounces) HERSHEY'S
    Unsweetened Baking
    Chocolate
¹/₄ cup butter or margarine

3 cups confectioners' sugar
1 teaspoon vanilla
¹/₈ teaspoon salt
¹/₃ cup milk

Melt baking chocolate and butter in small saucepan over very low heat, stirring constantly, until chocolate is melted and mixture is smooth. Pour into small mixer bowl; add confectioners' sugar, vanilla and salt. Blend in milk; beat to spreading consistency. (If frosting is too thick, add additional milk, 1 teaspoonful at a time, until frosting is desired consistency.)

About 2 cups frosting

CHOCOLATE WHIPPED CREAM

1 cup heavy or whipping cream
¹/₃ cup HERSHEY'S Syrup

2 tablespoons confectioners'
    sugar
¹/₂ teaspoon vanilla

Beat cream, syrup, confectioners' sugar and vanilla in small mixer bowl until soft peaks form. Especially good on cakes.   *About 2¹/₄ cups topping*

CHOCOLATE CREAM CHEESE FROSTING

3 packages (3 ounces each) cream
    cheese, softened
¹/₃ cup butter or margarine,
    softened

5 cups confectioners' sugar
1 cup HERSHEY'S Cocoa
5 to 7 tablespoons light cream

Blend cream cheese and butter in large mixer bowl. Combine confectioners' sugar and cocoa; add alternately with cream to cream cheese mixture. Beat to spreading consistency.   *About 3 cups frosting*

CHOCOLATE SATIN GLAZE

2 tablespoons sugar
2 tablespoons water

¹/₂ cup HERSHEY'S MINI CHIPS
    Semi-Sweet Chocolate

Combine sugar and water in small saucepan; cook over medium heat, stirring constantly, until mixture boils and sugar is dissolved. Remove from heat; immediately add MINI CHIPS Chocolates, stirring until melted. Continue stirring until glaze is desired consistency.   *About ¹/₂ cup glaze*

Index

Almonds
Butter Almond Crunch, 72
Chocolate-Almond Fudge, 68
Chocolate-Almond Tarts, 41
Chocolate Nut Sauce, 90

Bananas
Chocolate Banana Cream Pie, 39
Chocolate Chip Banana Bread, 78
Bar Cookies
Best Brownies, 48
Chocolate-Cherry Squares, 53
Peanut Butter Paisley Brownies, 48
Peanutty Chocolate Snack Squares, 85
Scrumptious Chocolate Layer Bars, 46
Bavarian Creams
Cocoa Bavarian Cream, 65
Strawberry-Chocolate Bavarian Cream, 59
Berry Cream, 21
Best Brownies, 48
Beverage: Microwave Hot Cocoa, 84
Black Bottom Pie, 38
Brandy Alexander Pie, 36
Breads
Chocolate Chip Banana Bread, 78
Chocolate Chip Bran Muffins, 83
Chocolate Chip Muffins, 79
Chocolate Chip Pancakes, 73
Chocolate Tea Bread, 79
Chocolate Waffles, 73
Cocoa Applesauce Muffins, 84
Butter Almond Crunch, 72

Cakes (*see also* **Tortes**)
Choco-Coconut Cake Roll, 10

Chocolate Peanut Butter Marble Cake, 32
Chocolate-Strawberry Chiffon Squares, 21
Chocolate Swirl Cake, 34
Chocolatetown Special Cake, 16
Cocoa Medallion Cake, 29
Cocoa-Spice Snackin' Cake, 16
Fudgey Pecan Cake, 33
Georgia Peach Shortcake, 12
Heavenly Heart Cake, 15
Lickety-Split Cocoa Cake, 20
Marble Chiffon Cake, 24
Mousse-Filled Cocoa Chiffon Cake, 26
Orange Cocoa Cake, 31
Picnic Medallion Cake, 29
Candies
Butter Almond Crunch, 72
Chocolate-Almond Fudge, 68
Chocolate Chip Nougat Log, 71
Chocolate Crackles, 86
Chocolate Rum Truffles, 69
Chocolate Truffles, 69
Cocoa Divinity, 69
Creamy Cocoa Taffy, 72
Double-Decker Fudge, 68
Easiest-Ever Cocoa Fudge, 85
Easy Rocky Road, 87
Fast Chocolate-Pecan Fudge, 87
Marshmallow-Nut Cocoa Fudge, 66
Nutty Rich Cocoa Fudge, 66
Rich Cocoa Fudge, 66
Cheesecakes
Chocolate Ricotta Cheesecake, 22
Cocoa Cheesecake, 32
Marble Cheesecake, 27
No-Bake Chocolate Cheesecake, 19

Party Chocolate Cheesecake Cups, 23
Strawberry Chocolate Chip Cheesecake, 20
Cherries
Cherry-Coconut Filling, 10
Chocolate-Cherry Squares, 53
Choco-Coconut Cake Roll, 10
Chocolate, forms of, 3–4
Chocolate-Almond Cream Filling, 9
Chocolate-Almond Fudge, 68
Chocolate-Almond Tarts, 41
Chocolate Banana Cream Pie, 39
Chocolate-Berry Parfaits, 64
Chocolate Buttercream Frosting, 92
Chocolate-Cherry Squares, 53
Chocolate Chip Banana Bread, 78
Chocolate Chip Bran Muffins, 83
Chocolate Chip Chocolate Cookies, 54
Chocolate Chip Muffins, 79
Chocolate Chip Nougat Log, 71
Chocolate Chip Pancakes, 73
Chocolate Chip Whole Wheat Cookies, 52
Chocolate-Coconut Frosting, 88
Chocolate Cookie Sandwiches, 52
Chocolate Crackles, 86
Chocolate Cream Cheese Frosting, 93
Chocolate Cream Filling, 41, 42
Chocolate Cream Frosting, 26
Chocolate Cream Pudding, 60
Chocolate Crumb Crust, 80
Chocolate-Filled Braid, 76
Chocolate-Filled Cream Puffs, 40
Chocolate Filling, 76
Chocolate Fudge Frosting, 92
Chocolate Ganache Glaze, 7

Chocolate Glaze, 42
Chocolate Mousse à l'Orange, 61
Chocolate Nut Sauce, 90
Chocolate Peanut Butter Marble Cake, 32
Chocolate-Peppermint Topping, 90
Chocolate Petal Crust, 36
Chocolate Ricotta Cheesecake, 22
Chocolate Rum Cream Pie, 35
Chocolate Rum Truffles, 69
Chocolate Satin Glaze, 93
Chocolate Sauce, 8
Chocolate-Strawberry Chiffon Squares, 21
Chocolate Swirl Cake, 34
Chocolate Tart Shells, 41
Chocolate Tea Bread, 79
Chocolate Truffles, 69
Chocolate Waffles, 73
Chocolate Whipped Cream, 93
Chocolatetown Cupcakes, 29
Chocolatetown Special Cake, 16
Classic Chocolate Cream Pie, 35
Cocoa Applesauce Muffins, 84
Cocoa Bavarian Cream, 65
Cocoa Brunch Rings, 74
Cocoa Cheesecake, 32
Cocoa Crumb Crust, 45
Cocoa Divinity, 69
Cocoa Glaze, 24
Cocoa Medallion Cake, 29
Cocoa-Pecan Kiss Cookies, 55
Cocoa-Spice Snackin' Cake, 16
Coconut
Choco-Coconut Cake Roll, 10
Chocolate-Coconut Frosting, 88
Macaroon Kiss Cookies, 49
Coffeecakes
Chocolate-Filled Braid, 76
Cocoa Brunch Rings, 74
Mocha-Chip Coffeecake, 77
Cold Mocha Soufflé, 62
Confectioners' Sugar Glaze, 76
Cookies
Chocolate Chip Chocolate Cookies, 54
Chocolate Chip Whole Wheat Cookies, 52
Chocolate Cookie Sandwiches, 52

Cocoa-Pecan Kiss Cookies, 55
Hershey's Great American Chocolate Chip Cookies, 51
Holiday Chocolate Cookies, 54
Macaroon Kiss Cookies, 49
Milk Chocolate Chip Cookies, 51
Reese's Chewy Chocolate Cookies, 51
Reese's Cookies, 55
Cozumel Whipped Cream, 63
Creamy Brownie Frosting, 48
Creamy Buttercream Frosting, 15
Creamy Cocoa Taffy, 72
Crème de Cacao Filling, 6
Crème de Cacao Pie, 82
Crème de Cacao Torte, 6
Creme-Filled Cupcakes, 28
Creme Filling, 52
Crumb-Nut Crust, 19
Crunch Topping, 84
Crusts
Chocolate Crumb Crust, 80
Chocolate Petal Crust, 36
Chocolate Tart Shells, 41
Cocoa Crumb Crust, 45
Crumb-Nut Crust, 19
Graham Cracker Crust, 38
Graham Crust, 23, 32
Pastry Crust, 20
Cupcakes
Chocolatetown Cupcakes, 29
Creme-Filled Cupcakes, 28

Decorator's Frosting, 54
Desserts, miscellaneous
Mocha Fudge Pudding Cake, 65
Peanut Butter Shells with Chocolate-Almond Cream, 9
Pears au Chocolat, 8
Double Chocolate Mousse, 59
Double-Decker Fudge, 68

Easiest-Ever Cocoa Fudge, 85
Easy Chocolate Mousse Pie, 38
Easy Hot Fudge Sauce, 87
Easy Rocky Road, 87

Fast Chocolate-Pecan Fudge, 87
Frostings
Berry Cream, 21
Chocolate Buttercream Frosting, 92

Chocolate-Coconut Frosting, 88
Chocolate Cream Cheese Frosting, 93
Chocolate Cream Frosting, 26
Chocolate Fudge Frosting, 92
Creamy Brownie Frosting, 48
Creamy Buttercream Frosting, 15
Decorator's Frosting, 54
Glossy Chocolate Sour Cream Frosting, 15
Orange Buttercream Frosting, 31
Quick Chocolate Frosting, 93
Vanilla Creme, 28
Fudge Brownie Pie, 45
Fudge Pecan Pie, 43
Fudge Walnut Pie, 43
Fudgey Pecan Cake, 33

Georgia Peach Shortcake, 12
Glazed Fruit, 23
Glazes: see **Toppings**
Glossy Chocolate Sour Cream Frosting, 15
Graham Cracker Crust, 38
Graham Crust, 23, 32
Graham Shells, 23

Heavenly Heart Cake, 15
Hershey's Great American Chocolate Chip Cookies, 51
Holiday Chocolate Cookies, 54
Hot Chocolate Soufflé, 56
Hot Fudge Sauce, 45, 9

Icings: see **Frostings**
Individual Fudge Soufflés, 60

Lickety-Split Cocoa Cake, 20

Macaroon Kiss Cookies, 49
Marble Cheesecake, 27
Marble Chiffon Cake, 24
Marshmallow-Nut Cocoa Fudge, 66
Melting Chocolate, 4
Mexican Cocoa Torte, 13
Microwave Recipes
Chocolate Chip Bran Muffins, 83
Chocolate Crackles, 86
Chocolate Crumb Crust, 80
Cocoa Applesauce Muffins, 84

Microwave Recipes *(cont.)*
Crème de Cacao Pie, 82
Easiest-Ever Cocoa Fudge, 85
Easy Hot Fudge Sauce, 87
Easy Rocky Road, 87
Fast Chocolate-Pecan Fudge, 87
Microwave Classic Chocolate Sauce, 85
Microwave Hershey Bar Mousse, 82
Microwave Hershey Bar Pie, 80
Microwave Hot Cocoa, 84
Peanutty Chocolate Snack Squares, 85
Milk Chocolate Chip Cookies, 51
Miniature Cream Puffs, 41
Mocha-Chip Coffeecake, 77
Mocha Fudge Pudding Cake, 65
Mousse-Filled Cocoa Chiffon Cake, 26
Mousses
Chocolate Mousse à l'Orange, 61
Double Chocolate Mousse, 59
Easy Chocolate Mousse Pie, 38
Microwave Hershey Bar Mousse, 82
Mt. Gretna Chocolate Fondue, 89

Napoleons, 42
No-Bake Chocolate Cheesecake, 19
Nutty Rich Cocoa Fudge, 66

Orange Buttercream Frosting, 31
Orange Cocoa Cake, 31
Orange Filling, 74

Pancakes: Chocolate Chip Pancakes, 73
Parfaits: Chocolate-Berry Parfaits, 64
Party Chocolate Cheesecake Cups, 23
Pastries
Chocolate-Almond Tarts, 41
Chocolate-Filled Cream Puffs, 40
Miniature Cream Puffs, 41
Napoleons, 42
Pastry Crust, 20

Peaches
Georgia Peach Shortcake, 12
Peach Topping, 19
Peanut Butter
Chocolate Peanut Butter Marble Cake, 32
Mt. Gretna Chocolate Fondue, 89
Peanut Butter Paisley Brownies, 48
Peanut Butter Shells with Chocolate-Almond Cream, 9
Reese's Chewy Chocolate Cookies, 51
Reese's Cookies, 55
Peanutty Chocolate Snack Squares, 85
Pears au Chocolat, 8
Pecans
Chocolate Nut Sauce, 90
Cocoa-Pecan Kiss Cookies, 55
Fast Chocolate-Pecan Fudge, 87
Fudge Pecan Pie, 43
Fudgey Pecan Cake, 33
Picnic Medallion Cake, 29
Pies
Black Bottom Pie, 38
Brandy Alexander Pie, 36
Chocolate Banana Cream Pie, 39
Chocolate Rum Cream Pie, 35
Classic Chocolate Cream Pie, 35
Crème de Cacao Pie, 82
Easy Chocolate Mousse Pie, 38
Fudge Brownie Pie, 45
Fudge Pecan Pie, 43
Fudge Walnut Pie, 43
Microwave Hershey Bar Pie, 80
Strawberry Chocolate Pie, 44
Puddings
Chocolate Cream Pudding, 60
Pots de Crème au Chocolat, 63

Quick Chocolate Frosting, 93

Reese's Chewy Chocolate Cookies, 51
Reese's Cookies, 55
Rich Cocoa Fudge, 66
Royal Glaze, 88

Sauces
Chocolate Nut Sauce, 90
Chocolate Sauce, 8
Easy Hot Fudge Sauce, 87
Hot Fudge Sauce, 45, 90
Microwave Classic Chocolate Sauce, 85
Mt. Gretna Chocolate Fondue, 89
Scrumptious Chocolate Layer Bars, 46
Soufflés
Cold Mocha Soufflé, 62
Hot Chocolate Soufflé, 56
Individual Fudge Soufflés, 60
Storing Chocolate, 5
Strawberries
Berry Cream, 21
Chocolate-Berry Parfaits, 64
Chocolate-Strawberry Chiffon Squares, 21
Strawberry-Chocolate Bavarian Cream, 59
Strawberry Chocolate Chip Cheesecake, 20
Strawberry Chocolate Pie, 44
Strawberry Topping, 45
Substituting Cocoa for Chocolate, 5

Toppings
Chocolate Ganache Glaze, 7
Chocolate Glaze, 42
Chocolate-Peppermint Topping, 90
Chocolate Satin Glaze, 93
Chocolate Whipped Cream, 93
Cocoa Glaze, 24
Confectioners' Sugar Glaze, 76
Cozumel Whipped Cream, 63
Glazed Fruit, 23
Peach Topping, 19
Royal Glaze, 88
Strawberry Topping, 45
Tortes
Crème de Cacao Torte, 6
Mexican Cocoa Torte, 13

Vanilla Creme, 28
Vanilla Frosting, 42

Waffles: Chocolate Waffles, 73
Walnuts: Fudge Walnut Pie, 43